Unsilenced

A MEMOIR OF HEALING
FROM TRAUMA

AMY J. GAMBLE

Unsilenced

ISBN-13: 979-8-218-31277-0

Published by SpeakUp4MentalHealth LLC

www.amygambleauthor.com

Please note that some of the names in this book have been changed to protect privacy. Any references to mental health treatment is the author's experience and may vary from person to person.

SpeakUp4MentalHealth LLC books are available at special discounts for bulk purchases in the U.S. by corporations, institutions, and other organizations. For more information, please contact Amy Gamble at speakup4mentalhealth@amygambleauthor.com

Cover design by: Miblart

Dedication

For all the women and men who may have been impacted by sexual abuse/assault and survived nonetheless. May you find strength in knowing *you are not alone.*

For my mother in heaven, who helped me find my voice. I'm eternally grateful for all the gifts you have blessed me with.

A Note to the Reader...

Some of the content in this book may be triggering for some people. The book contains scenes about bipolar disorder, PTSD, trauma, alcohol consumption, sexual abuse and assault and suicidal ideation.

Darkness comes upon my soul

My faith is weary and at foe

Send the angels once again

To save me in the night

My heart opens one more time

Ancient wisdom I seek to find

In the moment

Hope finds me!

~Amy Gamble

Chapter 1

It was a sweltering hot June day in 2006 with temperatures near 110 degrees in Phoenix, Arizona. It was easy to forget who I was as I lay on my stomach with my face in the desert dirt. The handcuffs were behind my back, cutting the flesh on my wrists. My lips sizzled on the surface of what seemed like hot lava rocks. The hair on my head was matted with a mixture of pool water and fine, powdered dirt.

I lifted my head and saw the cop's shoe inches from my face. His standard black service shoes with nylon shoestrings reminded me of Mr. Brock's shoes, one of the people who had sexually abused me. I cried out, "Please. Please don't hurt me." I remember the cop glancing down at me with a smug look. He uttered not one word of compassion or empathy.

After the cops dropped me to the ground, my older black lab Chance came up to my side, and with her usual way of greeting me, licked my face. It was as if the only sensible one around me was a four-legged dog.

When Chance touched my face, I remembered who I was, as her touch brought me back to the present moment. Then I realized I wasn't only the distraught woman lying on my stomach in the desert landscaping in front of my home. I was a forty-one-year-old former Olympic athlete, successful businesswoman, beloved daughter and sister, but I was living a real-life scene much better fit for high drama theatrics and far away from the safety of my family's home in West Virginia.

My immediate family consisted of my father, mom, three

1

sisters—Shelley, Sherry, and Cindy—and my cousin Bonnie who lived with us after her mother died. My sisters and cousin were all significantly older than I was. Shelley and Sherry were twins and were nine years older than me. Cindy was seven years older, and Bonnie six years older. It was more like growing up with five mothers who were trying to tell me what to do. Like every family, we weren't perfect, however, they almost always supported me. Whether it was attending my sporting events and cheering loudly from the sidelines, taking me to USA basketball tryouts and other basketball camps in Georgia and North Carolina, or attending my piano recitals, someone was always behind me cheering me on. Later in life, we vacationed together, and my family frequently visited me in the eight out of nine different cities I lived in. It's fair to say we were all pretty close.

But my family was nowhere in sight in the Arizona desert.

Tears welled up in my eyes, clouding my vision. Then they overflowed, slowly dripping down my face falling into Chance's fur. I said, "Hi, Chancie," as she rubbed her head against mine and made her usual high-pitched whining noise. I leaned my forehead on her head and found a moment of comfort with the kind of love only a dog knows. It was a moment of pleasantness in an otherwise tragic experience.

As I neared the end of an ugly crying bout, I was trembling and shaking in the same way I'd done for months prior. I was having a flashback and a psychotic episode. It's not unheard of for someone who has experienced a great deal of trauma to have a psychotic break. It's underreported because the blame generally gets assigned to some other mental health condition, and I was diagnosed with bipolar disorder. Perhaps it could have been the trauma triggering mania which resulted in psychosis.

But trauma and flashbacks had been dogging me for over six months. One of them would begin with my head and body shaking violently, as if I were having a seizure. As I'd shake and tremble, my head would itch. I would shake my hair, and I could feel bodily sensations from pain inflicted on me. I could feel the grass prickling against my skin. I felt pure terror for as long as the flashback lasted. Once it was over, I was exhausted. However, I was back in the present moment and completely aware of my surroundings.

This particular flashback with grass making my skin crawl reoccurred frequently and took me back to my sister Sherry's wedding day, when one of the groomsmen raped me.

I was fifteen years old.

I remember that day well. It was a beautiful, intense, sunny day for an outdoor wedding, though it was unbearably humid. The kind of humidity that makes your hair droop and feels like a hot steam sauna. The private estate on top of a hill had a two-story Victorian style house that was set back several yards away from the pool and tennis court. The pool didn't have any water in it. I distinctly remember seeing the cracked white plaster crinkled up on the bottom of it.

After the wedding was over, the champagne flowed vigorously and the shoulder of beef was cooking on a giant-sized skewer in an outdoor fire pit. I was so thirsty I guzzled down my glass of champagne and asked for another. I was dehydrated from lack of water and sweating profusely. By the time the beef finished cooking, I was more than tipsy and had unknowingly become a target for a man nearly twice my age.

It was about dusk, and I went to the front of the grounds and was standing by a bench near the tennis court. He came over to me and coaxed me to sit on his lap. He pulled me closer to him with one hand, as the other hand clung to his beer can. He sloppily kissed me. I tried to get up, but he pulled me back down and reached his hand under my dark pink bridesmaid gown.

I stood up. The next thing I remember is being in his truck. I can see my sister Shelley chasing after the truck, throwing her hands in the air and yelling, "Amy, come back! Don't go!" It was as if she knew his intentions.

He sped backward down the driveway and then took me down a long dirt road. We were far away from the dancing and singing of the wedding reception. Before I knew it, I was in the tall, itchy grass, flat on my back. It would only be the next day when I could see and feel what had happened the night before.

That memory became stuck in my mind and came out as a haunting flashback, yet somehow always sparing me from his final violent act. But I would end up reliving the terror I'd felt through unwanted flashbacks and the aftermath of emotions that got trapped somewhere in my mind and eventually came out in one way or another.

~

On that hot summer day in Phoenix, the police officers couldn't see the hurting victim stuck in a time warp, crying out for help. All they saw was a woman shattered. All they knew was how this woman tried to push the 6'4" ex-Marine who cleaned her pool. All they heard was about this woman who tried to pull her friend Jan into the pool. Jan panicked and screamed at the pool man to call the police.

When the police came, I was swimming in the pool, what would have otherwise been a nice activity on a hot June day. But I was not well. I was laughing and singing "Amazing Grace."

The officers walked up to the edge of the pool. "Do you want to come swimming?" I asked. They both answered no.

I got out of the pool and stood next to the officer. I was wearing a tee-shirt and knee level shorts. They were soaked, clinging to my legs and heavy from the pool water. He grabbed my arm immediately and said, "Let's go, Amy. You're coming with us."

I took a step back, pulled my arm from his grasp. He let go easily. I sat down with my legs and arms crossed, as if I were protesting. That's when the two police officers decided to "carry" me through my house and the front yard to where their police car was parked. It was more like dragging a limp one hundred eighty pounds of dead weight. I didn't resist or fight as they moved me across the desert landscaping with rocks and cactus scraping my body.

When we got to the police car, the officers tried to put me in the backseat. Even though I was handcuffed behind my back, my self-defense training kicked in, and I fought like my life depended on it. I leveraged my body weight against the door frame as my legs continuously moved, pushing all of us backward away from the car. There was no way I was getting in the backseat of that car. That's what self-defense training taught me. Because the moment they got you in the vehicle, your chance of survival went down significantly.

At the time, I thought the police were a threat to me. In my mind, I was a victim. I was having flashbacks, and I was delusional. One moment I thought I was an angel, and the next I was lying in that tall grass, horrified. Later I would learn what I did was called "resisting arrest." But at the time, I had no idea I was being arrested. What had I done?

After a few minutes, the officers grew tired of fighting with me. They dropped me face down on my stomach and called the fire department. I don't know why they didn't call for an ambulance. It makes me wonder if some part of them knew I needed medical attention, but not for physical health, for mental health. Looking back, it also makes me sad to think how I was treated.

I don't think either of them was trained in Crisis Intervention Training (CIT), a special training offered to law enforcement officers to learn how to handle people who are experiencing a mental health crisis. The first CIT was developed in Memphis in 1998, though it was not widely adopted by every police department across the United States.

Categorically, a mental health crisis is when a person's behavior puts them at risk for hurting themselves or someone else or if they are unable to care for themselves. I met those criteria.

I doubt police officers in my neighborhood thought they needed CIT. It was a place where the multi-million-dollar houses stood elegantly quiet on a bluff. It wasn't every day this neighborhood saw so much excitement. It was the type of place where seeing a neighbor was fairly unusual, much less police cars and firetrucks.

In my moment of lucid thinking, I heard the firetruck siren. I took a deep breath and sighed with relief. Finally, someone was coming to help me and not hurt me.

I was crying but very calm when the fireman approached me. I was still lying face down, struggling like a turtle stuck on its back.

"Are you okay?" the fireman asked as he approached me.

"My lips are burnt from the rocks and I have cactus needles in my arm," I replied.

"What's your name?"

"Amy Gamble," I answered.

"We are going to check your vital signs. Okay?" he said with compassion and kindness.

The fireman helped me get turned around and sat me up in about as comfortable a position as one can achieve when handcuffed behind her back. He took a soft cloth and gently wiped my face. My salty tears had dripped across the burns on my lips, and even in my state of mind, I could feel the pain.

The fireman took my blood pressure, checked my vitals, and spoke softly to me in a calming voice. His approach with me completely deescalated the situation, something the police could have done with the proper training.

After a brief period of time, the fireman motioned to the police officers that I was medically okay.

"Are you taking me to the hospital?" I asked.

One of the police officers came back over to me and put his hand around my arm and squeezed it tightly. He said in a patronizing voice, "Let's go, Amy. Get in the back of the car. Don't give us any trouble."

I walked over to the car and got in the backseat. Instead of sending me to the hospital in an ambulance, the police officers were hell bent on taking me to jail.

Several months later, I had a conversation with my friend Chuck about what happened on that dreadful day. As my luck would have it, the fireman was the husband of a job recruiter who had helped me obtain my last marketing position with a pharmaceutical company. I found out months later from Chuck she knew what happened to me. She asked Chuck if I was doing better. I was mortified and embarrassed someone from my professional world knew a piece of my story. I was sure she'd think I was "crazy."

~

It was the end of summer in 2005 when I first met Susan. It was another scorching hot, big blue-sky day in Phoenix where the lizards ran up the backyard walls that fenced in my five-bedroom home equipped with a pool, hot tub, and outdoor fireplace. I had lived in my comfortable home for nearly two years with my three dogs—Chance, Shasta, and Buddy. I had purchased the house after landing a marketing manager position with a large pharmaceutical company. It was also the first house I bought by myself, after ending a ten-year relationship with my partner, Alexis.

Even though I had frequent visits from my family and my good friend Samantha, I was alone most of the time. When I wasn't traveling for work, I spent most of my time in my home office. A couple of my friends thought I needed to get out and meet other people. They talked me into going to dinner so I could meet Susan. Susan had recently finished graduate school with a master's in business. My friends thought I could be a mentor for Susan and help her develop her professional career.

I remember the day I met her as if that occurrence happened yesterday. I was upstairs working in my home office and attempting to catch up on the slew of unread and redundant emails. I could feel my chest tighten from anxiety caused from a combination of too many work demands mixed with an overwhelming desire to please other people. Or the "disease to please," as Oprah Winfrey calls it.

I glanced down at my watch, and in that moment, I thought I should just call and tell my friends I couldn't make it. And then I talked myself into going for dinner anyhow. A decision I would come to regret.

Driving over to the restaurant, I ran my hand through my hair numerous times as I often did when I was anxious. I would come to learn years later anxiety was a precursor to hypomania, and with my mind racing with all sorts of thoughts, mostly about work, I know without a shadow of doubt I was hypomanic. My obsessive paranoia had kicked in, and it had a way of relentlessly taking hold of me. A few years prior, I had been diagnosed with bipolar disorder, and one of the symptoms I experienced when not taking the right combination of medications was paranoia. At that time, I didn't have the words or knowledge to be able to describe what I was feeling. But looking back, I know this paranoia interfered with my ability to trust my own instincts.

I was under the treatment of a psychiatrist for bipolar disorder, but I had yet to really understand how the symptoms impacted me. In my limited understanding of bipolar disorder, I couldn't quite fit myself into one of the boxes. The manner in which I came to be diagnosed was complicated. At this point in my life, I didn't fully understand the difference between what were symptoms and what was a part of my personality. I was always a high energy person, fairly creative, intelligent, and very goal oriented and driven. The books I was reading about bipolar disorder were now telling me "goal directed behaviors" was one of the symptoms of bipolar disorder. In my mind, I was thinking, "I'm an Olympian, of course I have goal directed behaviors."

Then there were descriptions of "high levels of creativity," and even intelligence being common traits of people who have bipolar. It felt to me like all my talents, skills, and qualities were being labeled as a mental illness, and that didn't sit well with me. It made me feel ashamed. I simply couldn't understand it.

In addition to my lack of understanding about symptoms, I was still not entirely convinced my diagnosis was correct. It seemed any time I saw a new doctor, the diagnosis would change between bipolar disorder, post-traumatic stress disorder, and anxiety. Even though I still had my doubts, I took my medications as prescribed.

It was only in retrospect that I realized it wasn't the right combination of medications that I needed. Without being able to articulate symptoms to my doctor, she couldn't really help me. It's not like she had a blood test she could take and determine exactly what medications or dosages might work. There was plenty of research on medications for bipolar disorder, but mental health treatment is still very much a trial-and-error scenario.

"Try this medication and see how you feel."

"Oh, that medication didn't make you feel right, so try this one."

So, on the day I crossed paths with Susan, it wasn't my best day. I was far from trusting my instincts and not in a position to cautiously judge someone's character. But I noticed something was off with Susan. I didn't know what it was, but I knew something wasn't quite right. She seemed very loud and somewhat immature for someone who was thirty-two years old. I ignored my internal warning signal, otherwise known as a "gut instinct." Despite Susan's negative vibe, she was brilliant. She thought of herself as an authority on many topics and certainly came across as if she knew what she was talking about. She was very confident, maybe even a bit arrogant. While I disliked a lot of arrogance, I've always been intrigued and drawn to really smart people. I could kind of look past qualities I didn't care for, because I always believed no one was perfect. I had an unbalanced habit of looking for the good in people and discounting myself about anything I might not like.

A few weeks after I met Susan, I invited her to get together for coffee. I discounted my own judgement and gut feelings about Susan. I rationalized I'd only seen her once and was probably just reading too much into her personality. She did seem very interesting, so I thought what could possibly hurt by talking with her.

We sat in a local coffee shop talking intensely for a few hours. We seemed to have many things in common, though varying viewpoints about people.

At some point, Susan blurted, "I've had therapy for sexual abuse."

I glanced back at her, not at all shocked because I knew how common sexual violence was against women. I replied matter of factly, "I've been sexually abused, too. Good for you for getting help."

It wasn't the first time I had ever mentioned I was sexually abused to someone other than my family. I had general conversations over the years with other friends. I never provided much detail on my end, but I did listen to other friends' stories. Susan seemed to take the conversation to an entirely different level.

Susan suddenly shifted her eyes, stiffened her back, tilted her head forward and changed her tone, saying, "You really need to get help for that. There's a lot that's wrong with you."

I remember looking at her, stunned. I'd only seen Susan twice and wasn't sure what I was seeing, but I had studied non-verbal communication in college, and it sure looked like this was a person who had dramatic shifts in facial expressions and piercing eye contact. Her expressions looked like she was angry. Her brow creased with intensity, and her brown eyes glared at me. My stomach was churning, my chest was tightening, and my head felt dizzy, and even with all those uncomfortable warning signs, I still listened to Susan.

She went on to tell me to find a therapist who specialized in sexual abuse counseling. My fast-moving mind had already gone to trying to figure out how I could "fix" myself. No matter how much I'd accomplished, I was always searching for ways to improve. If there was something wrong with me, I was going to figure out a way to fix it. It never dawned on me that Susan didn't know me well enough to tell me in so many words *you are broken.*

I don't remember everything Susan said to me, but I do remember how she made me feel. I felt a cloud of shame come over me, as if I was dirty. Had I done something bad? That was how I felt. Even though she had a similar experience to me, she turned the table and seemed non-compassionate. Later I would learn her body language and tone of voice triggered my PTSD.

It seems she enjoyed being the person "in the know." She spoke with great authority when it came to sexual assault and mental health conditions, though she acted as if she had healed her inner demons. But instead of gently offering suggestions or being cautious with what she had come to learn, she seemed to enjoy the power trip of being the all-knowing person. The one who had it all figured out.

Honestly, in the end, I felt responsible for allowing Susan to influence me. I went against my gut feeling, which told me to stay away from her. However, I was the one who reached out and invited her to coffee. I was the one who trusted her with something very personal. I never expected her to make me feel like a child, but that's what happened when I was unknowingly "triggered." And Susan knew exactly what was happening. She had worked for a few years in a mental health treatment facility for children and adolescents. Over coffee, Susan had been saying, "I like to mess with people's minds. It's so easy, you know. They're just a bunch of wackos!" And even with this very blatant warning sign, I ignored my inner voice. I believe a part of me simply thought she was joking. And another part didn't understand trauma enough to realize what was happening to me.

The very next day after meeting with Susan, I started searching the Internet for a therapist who specialized in sexual abuse counseling. I found a very comprehensive website with lots of information, and I made the call to Belinda, a call that changed the course of my life.

Chapter 2

Before my first visit with Belinda in October 2005, Susan dropped off a set of watercolor paints and paper. She suggested I start using them to help me cope with memories. Though I had seen Susan a few times prior, she decided she wanted to keep her distance from me because from Susan's perspective as I embarked upon healing from sexual abuse, the therapy would be very intense. She felt as if I needed privacy and the space to process the emotions that may come up. At the time, although it was unwarranted, I felt shame creep up. As if all of a sudden I had something so wrong with me, like I was no longer going to be any fun to be around.

I hadn't a clue what Susan was talking about, but I was willing to try just about anything to help myself. It had been many years since the sexual assaults had occurred, and I hadn't given much thought as to how all this trauma may have impacted me. I started using the watercolors as soon as I got them. Painting and drawing were never among my talents, but I found I could disconnect easily as I painted, never really knowing what was going to come out of my subconscious mind.

I also purchased a book Susan suggested, called *The Courage to Heal*, by Ellen Bass and Laura Davis. Instead of taking baby steps, I approached healing from sexual abuse as if it were any other thing I tried to accomplish—goal oriented with a time frame. I immersed myself in learning about sexual assault, and I started to explore how it had impacted me.

Not realizing what I was asking of myself, I dove right into intensive therapy, as a couple of weeks after I first started using the watercolors, I had my first appointment with Belinda. I set out to find her office about forty-five minutes across town from where I lived.

As I drove into the parking lot, I saw a bookstore across the street. I thought it may be a good place to stop after therapy. I noticed Belinda's office was in an aging corporate building. Considering many buildings in Phoenix were relatively new, older, more run-down buildings had a way of standing out. The overall area didn't have a good "feel" to it. Then again, my stomach was quite nervous about going to sexual abuse therapy, so any uneasiness I felt could have been attributed to my own feelings about what I was doing.

As I got out of the car, I kept questioning myself on why I needed therapy for sexual abuse. Then I thought about my conversation with Susan, and she seemed to believe therapy was necessary. I wasn't entirely convinced, as I had been very successful in overcoming my childhood traumas. But I didn't think about my strengths in that moment; I thought about my weaknesses. Looking back, I know it was a fundamental mistake.

I slowly walked up the steps to the second floor and found Belinda's office. I knocked on the door, and she answered.

"Hi there. Are you Amy?"

"Yes, I'm Amy Gamble. I had an appointment with you today."

"Come on in," Belinda said, opening the door wide.

I walked into the office, and the first thing I noticed was her long hair flowing like a white stallion mane. I then looked down and saw her administrative desk a few steps on the left by the door. She had a loveseat in front of the desk and a high back chair against the window. Her whiteboard was directly in front of the loveseat. I wondered, "What the heck is that for?" It felt like a safe space, but pretty crammed with furniture.

She stood a couple inches shorter than my 5'10" frame. The first order of business was to fill out the intake forms. When I got to the section on mental health diagnosis, I intentionally left it blank. One of the many suggestions from Susan was she thought there was no way I could have bipolar disorder. That was exactly what I wanted to hear, so I embraced the idea.

I was also afraid Belinda would have some kind of bias if I said I had bipolar disorder. I wanted her to work with me and decide for herself what disorder I had or didn't have. I never told her I was taking medication or that I was seeing Dr. Tracy, a psychiatrist. It had been six years since I had been initially diagnosed with bipolar disorder. I had been seeing Dr. Tracy for about two years before I started seeing Belinda. My approach with Belinda was clearly not the best way to go about starting a therapeutic relationship, and I wouldn't recommend doing what I did.

At first, it was really unclear to me why I needed therapy for sexual abuse. I had successfully been able to block out and compartmentalize most of my traumatic experiences for the greater part of my life. Years later, I would learn every survivor has different ways of coping with sexual assault. Some people seek out therapy, some people chose to ignore it ever happened or put it in the back of their mind. Some people have mental breakdowns. There's not a one-size-fits-all approach for dealing with it.

In my case, there were signs my subconscious was trying to tell me. When we would have annual meetings for work, we would often be in a large ballroom with hundreds of people. On the round tables, they always had a couple of pitchers of water, notepads, and pens. Year after year during those annual meetings, some people would doodle on their pads. I would always fill up my page with a picture of a man, unshaven and with a mustache. I never thought anything of it until one day a colleague asked me, "Amy, why do you draw that man all over your paper?" I had no idea why.

Many years after I first began therapy for sexual abuse, I would discover how all this emotional "stuffing" had an impact on me. I read in a book that memories could hurt my mental and physical health. I had struggled for years with endometriosis and polycystic ovarian disease, eventually leading to a hysterectomy by the time I was forty. Female problems historically ran in my family. But there's also research that demonstrates gynecologic problems are common among women who are survivors of childhood sexual abuse. I was always battling in my own mind against becoming a statistic, but this one was irrefutable.

The memories that were causing my emotional and physical problems were not conscious. They were not top of mind. I only thought of them when someone brought up the topic. I would later find out they were much closer to the surface than I had realized, and I would come to learn how the impact of the trauma affected me.

After a few "get to know me" general therapy sessions, Belinda went to the whiteboard to teach me about my "parent," "adult," and "child" ego states.

"We all have different ego states that can come out at any time during social interactions," Belinda said. "Each person has a 'parent,' 'adult,' and 'child' side to ourselves. Becoming aware of what part is coming to the surface, you can better learn how to take more control over your thoughts and behaviors."

"I think that's kind of fascinating," I said sincerely, as I had always been interested in psychology and never really heard about what Belinda was teaching me.

"Your child side is responsible for imagination and play. This is important to realize because sometimes your child self wants to play and your parent side needs to step in and make sure you're only playing when you're supposed to be playing."

"I can see what you're saying." I nodded.

"If you had a bad parent, you're more likely to talk to yourself more harshly," Belinda continued. "Most importantly, as a childhood sexual abuse survivor, you need to know when you get triggered and you have a childlike response, you need to grow yourself up and get into your adult self. You'll need to learn your triggers so you can do this."

"Oh. I never realized any of this before," I said, attempting to apply the information I was learning to my life. It felt overwhelming because I had never given any thought to how being sexually abused had affected me.

Belinda went on to explain the impact of childhood sexual abuse on ego states. I slouched my shoulders and sank deeper into the loveseat, as I suddenly recognized I wasn't immune to the devastating effects of sexual abuse. It was more than an ah-ha moment. I could feel the realization of what I was learning come over me like a wave. It nearly took my breath away.

When the therapy sessions were more general, like everyday

issues of anxiety or a discussion of coping strategies, I was fine, as I had seen a therapist in the past for a couple of years and knew what to expect. But when Belinda started to talk about the impact of sexual abuse and started having me recall my experiences, I seemed to have difficulty. She started questioning me about my past and asked me to sit down on the floor and show her the watercolors I had brought with me.

"Whatcha got there, Amy? Did you bring your watercolors for me?" Belinda said with curiosity.

"I did bring some of my watercolors," I answered.

"Why don't you tell me all about them?" Belinda said, gesturing for me to sit down. She sat on the edge of her tall, wide-back chair and leaned forward.

I laid the watercolor drawings on the floor and sat down. It felt kind of weird to sit on the floor because it made me feel small and powerless.

One picture I had painted was filled up with pairs of eyes. Brown eyes.

Belinda asked, "What do all those eyes mean?"

"I don't know," I said quietly.

"How do you decide what to paint?"

"I just sit down and let my subconscious paint whatever it wants to."

"Why don't you tell me about the sexual abuse you experienced."

"What do you want to know?" I asked nervously.

"When were you first sexually abused?" Belinda asked, leaning forward.

"The earliest I can remember is six years old," I answered, becoming more uncomfortable.

"Can you tell me what happened?"

I answered Belinda's questions easily and without any emotion, as I had significant recall of the when, where, how, and who of the sexual abuse I experienced. Looking back, sometimes I think she retraumatized me with her therapeutic approach, and at the time this made me feel awkward and uncomfortable.

On the day in therapy when Belinda took me back to my past to revisit the sexual abuse, it was a pleasant eighty-degree day in December. Pleasant on the outside, but miserable in my heavy heart, troubled mind, and saddened soul. The combination of reviewing the watercolors and revisiting the past overwhelmed me. I could feel my body quivering, knee bouncing, and foot thumping up and down. I had to get out of there. Reflecting, I know my PTSD was triggered.

Four weeks into therapy, and I had become an emotional wreck. On that day I got in my car and started to cry uncontrollably. I blasted the air conditioning and put my hands on the steering wheel, grasping it like it was some kind of lifeline. I slammed my eyes shut and squeezed them closed because the sunlight felt like someone was pouring boiling water on me.

As I drove out of the parking lot talking out loud, my hands suddenly reached up to my throat as if to choke myself. At this point, my entire body was shaking. I was sitting at a red light in gut-wrenching emotional pain, seeing through a flashback where my cousin, Ron, sits on top of me, choking me as I gasped for breath. The flashback was so vivid it felt like the trauma was happening in the present moment, even though there was a part of me that was aware of where I was. It was almost like watching a dual screen television with two different channels playing at one time.

That day in therapy was the real, bona fide opening of Pandora's Box. Whatever was holding all my traumatic memories in a safe place in my brain had now lain open every scar, scab, and callus I had built up. The floodgates were officially open, and my life was going to get a whole lot harder before it got better.

In fairness to the therapist, there was no way she could have known my history when I walked through her door. Her practice was specifically set up to focus on victims of sexual abuse, and I knew what service she was offering. Taking a step to go to sexual abuse therapy was an indicator I was ready for that type of personal exploration, although I can honestly say I had no idea what I was getting into, and Belinda never gave me any pamphlets or handouts to shed light on this type of therapy. To be honest, I'm not so certain it would have mattered.

At the time, I had very little knowledge about post-traumatic stress disorder (PTSD), and I had no real insight of how all the trauma I had experienced in my life was affecting me. I wasn't able to articulate what had happened to me in a nice neat package with a bow on top. I wasn't at a place of being able to have a greater understanding of my traumas, and most importantly, the impact trauma had on me—physically, emotionally, and spiritually. All this would take years of hard work and a tremendous amount of inner strength to fight through the often-painful realizations.

Four sexual assaults existed as a big blind spot in my psyche. All of them had occurred by the time I was sixteen. I was disconnected emotionally from those experiences. The memories were buried. I think they had to be in order for me to have survived and thrived in the way that I did. I learned in studying the effects of trauma that the "thinking brain" actually goes off-line during a traumatic experience. It shuts down. This contributes to not being able to assign words to the trauma, until later working through it in therapy or in self-reflection.

While working with Belinda, in retrospect, I told her about the watercolors, and she seemed intrigued. Her interest seemed to come from a place of curiosity and maybe from less of a place of therapeutic value. Belinda also had me revisit my past at a pace that was simply too fast for me, and because of this I was flooded with memories and unprocessed emotions.

I later learned it's not always necessary to tell a therapist detail about a trauma. For some people, this can be retraumatizing. As a person who had successfully been able to block out the trauma, it definitely retraumatized me. And by asking me specific questions about the abuse, it opened doors to my past that had been closed for decades. I feel like there may have been a safer approach Belinda could have taken.

I think it would have been helpful to focus on how I could recognize a trigger and focus on changing my behavior in the present, without reflecting back to the actual sexual abuse in gross detail. I don't think I necessarily needed to know a deep psychological analysis of the how and why I became "smaller" in certain situations. Then again, I'm not completely sure I could have healed without understanding the "whys," as painful as that process of discovery became.

As time passed, I would learn how a trigger could cause me to feel like I was the age of whenever the traumatic event had happened. The feeling may have lasted a few minutes or sometimes longer. It may have shown up as sort of a cowering type of gesture or an inability to react to a situation as my adult self. These were some of the effects of sexual abuse that I was completely unaware were happening in my life, but would later learn about. I was deeply disappointed and discouraged when I discovered this. Even though I had a high level of self-awareness, I had some blind spots that made me vulnerable. When I took an inventory of my life journey, I felt shame and embarrassment at certain encounters that stood out in my mind, although I knew it wasn't my fault. And as I began to realize how the sexual abuse had impacted me, I also felt a great deal of anger, which was dispersed in my mind to a lot of different people.

But Belinda managed to rip all the Band-Aids off of me in a matter of a few sessions. I'm left to wonder, would a more skilled therapist have done the same?

~

My long, miserable June day with the cops by my side would continue as we took the less than ten-minute ride from my house to the police station. We arrived in the middle of the afternoon with the sun beating down in full intensity, tipping the temperature gauge at over 105 degrees. The cops got out and left me in the back of the car. In frustration and confusion, I slammed my head on the glass partition separating the backseat from the front. It hurt. After sitting there for a while without air conditioning and no windows down, I leaned over and fell asleep. The saving grace was my clothes were soaking wet from being in the pool. And those wet clothes provided a way for my body to stay cool.

The next thing I remember is the shoe cop saying, "She disappeared. Where did she go?" followed by laughter. I was glad the cop came back to get me out of the car, and I was somewhat groggy because I had been sleeping. My head was hurting, and I felt as if I were in some kind of fog. I wondered where they were taking me now.

He opened the car door, and I sort of stumbled to get my balance. I could feel the heat from the black pavement as the sun reflected off of it. There weren't any cars moving around, and I didn't see another soul. As we walked up to the building, I was surprised at how small it was. He opened the door and led me into a tiny jail cell. I noticed a woman standing in the right corner of the room with her head down and her hands fidgeting with papers. I was calm and peaceful until, with my hands behind my back, he handcuffed me to the cement block in the cell. Later I would learn from the police report that he went to such great measures to restrain me because he was fearful I might hurt myself. Instead of keeping me calm, it sent me into full-blown hysterics.

From my perspective, I was a woman who had been experiencing flashbacks pertaining to sexual violence, and then I was restrained and completely vulnerable. What a horrible thing to do to someone experiencing mental distress, especially when there were other alternatives, like taking me directly to the hospital and getting me the mental health treatment I so desperately needed.

In the jail cell, I began singing "Amazing Grace" at the top of my lungs. I called the female dispatcher in the back room with me the devil. I even went so far as to ask her directly if she was the devil. I screamed, "In the name of the Father, the Son, and the Holy Spirit, God help me!"

After a while, I wore myself out. My friend Jan walked into the police station, and they let her come to the cell to see me. I later learned she was advocating with the police to take me to a psychiatric hospital.

She asked, "Amy, are you okay? I'm really worried about you."

"Get me out of here," I pleaded.

Then, as quickly as she appeared, she was gone again. I don't know how long I sat in that cell, but I know it was long enough for the air conditioning to cause me to shiver. Now the wet clothes were a hindrance. I was so thirsty, tired, and confused.

The cop who brought me into the station came by, and I pleaded with him to take off the handcuffs.

He asked, "Are you going to behave?"

"Yes. I'll behave," I replied. "Can I have a drink of water?"

"Yes, you can have a drink."

He brought me a plastic cup of water and put it up to my mouth to help me drink it. And then a little while later he removed the handcuffs. It was a moment of compassion with limited understanding of how much I was suffering.

I'd never been in jail before. My only encounter with law enforcement came from a speeding ticket, except for one other time in my life when I had a psychotic episode and the deputy sheriff came to my mother's home to involuntarily commit me. I had been diagnosed and subsequently undiagnosed with bipolar disorder in the winter of 1999. I was living in Philadelphia and working as a director of marketing for a large pharmaceutical company at the time.

One psychiatrist said I had bipolar disorder, and another dumped out my medications into a trash can in front of me and told me I didn't have it. What was I supposed to think? I didn't want to have a mental illness, so anyone who told me I didn't have one would be the person I focused on listening to.

In July of 2001, my father's death triggered mania, and the lack of sleep for days on end led to psychosis. I was not taking any medication for bipolar disorder.

My father had brain cancer and we chose to keep him at his home and take care of him. I was living in Arizona at the time but took off work to come help my mother care for him.

His condition became so bad he was bedridden and couldn't talk. I was the person who sat beside his bed late into the night and held his hand. I would say, "Daddy, it's me, Amy. I'm going to read some passages from your Shriner's book." He would squeeze my hand in approval and look at me with his left, big blue eye. Before reading to him, I'd pause for a moment and feel my tears slowly well up. I tried to hold it together and be strong for my dad. But it was an extremely stressful time.

The next day, when he died, the caregiver who was helping my family came to me and asked me to close his eyes. I was resistant and didn't want to do that, but I did, and it all became very traumatic. I suppose it was because I had PTSD and it was another collection of traumatic events added to my list.

After the funeral, I was having a full-blown manic episode. It took only a couple of days before I had a psychotic episode. My bipolar disorder diagnosis may have been confusing to the psychiatrists I encountered; however, it was not a surprise to my family. My mother had been diagnosed with bipolar when I was nineteen and had just finished my freshman year of school and playing basketball at the University of Tennessee.

In September 1985, a few weeks before I left to go train for the Olympics, my sister Sherry was hospitalized and diagnosed with bipolar disorder. Later, I would learn about the strong genetic risk factor for bipolar disorder. There's no doubt it runs in my family.

On the day I had the psychotic episode at my family's home in West Virginia, they knew what to do to get help for me. There was no big drama or handcuffs. I simply walked to the sheriff's car and got in the back. The sheriff's deputy bought me a fish sandwich and diet Pepsi, then dropped me off at the hospital.

The only question I remember asking the deputy sheriff was, "Are you the good guys or the bad guys?"

"We're the good guys!" he said very positively, then proceeded to treat me with dignity and respect as my mind reeled with confusion.

I learned there are advantages to living in a small town versus a big city. In a small town, many people knew my family. In a big city, no one knew me. In a small town, I was treated with loving compassion and respect in one of my most vulnerable moments.

On the other hand, in June 2006, the day I had a psychotic episode and landed with my face planted in the desert dirt in the big city, I had an earlier interaction with police. They picked me up wandering the streets in downtown Phoenix during rush hour traffic. I had my three dogs with me and had abandoned my vehicle. In my confused state of mind, I was having a delusion where I thought I was an angel sent to help people because the world was ending. I unfortunately vividly remember walking in front of cars thinking I was invisible and could walk right through them. It's sometimes hard for me to imagine my brain could let me down so hard.

The police put my dogs in the back of the police car with me and drove my car home. They called a crisis team to come out and evaluate me. At that point, they concluded I wasn't a danger to myself or others and therefore didn't need mental health treatment. The Crisis Team was a part of an agency which, in theory, would be called out to assist police officers when there was a mental health crisis situation. If the Crisis Team had done their job correctly and taken me to get mental health treatment, they could have saved me more unnecessary trauma. The incident with my friend Jan and the ex-Marine would never have happened, much less the unfortunate situation in the jail cell. All of it could have been avoided.

But was it my fault it happened in the first place? As much as I'd like to blame other people, I held myself accountable for not being a better student of the mental health conditions I have. On one hand, I wanted to take all the blame for what happened to me, and on the other hand, I got frustrated knowing the people who were entrusted to help me instead failed me. A part of me felt as if I were a victim of the mental health treatment system and its many failures. Another part of me wanted to hold accountable those who sexually assaulted me and caused me so much trauma. In time, I would have to come to terms with all those different perspectives.

~

After hours of being held in the jail cell, the cops finally took me to a mental health crisis center for treatment. They gave me some high-powered medications and released me after about forty-eight hours. There's no way that was long enough to stabilize me. To say I received mental health treatment is a stretch, but the bar is so low for the term "treatment," an ant couldn't crawl under it. It's really an unacceptable system.

For me, the game of survival of the fittest was on. I was going to have to find my way without much help.

Chapter 3

While I was in the crisis treatment center, my mother and Christy, one of my cousins on my mother's side of the family, flew out to Arizona to help support me. It had only been a few days since I was released from the crisis center, but my head had cleared enough to try to start looking after my best interest.

The flashbacks had subsided, probably with the help of medications, but I'm not sure. I attempted to get in touch with the psychiatrist I had been seeing, but she refused to see me because I had missed a few appointments. I wasn't sure where to go for outpatient treatment, so I got in touch with Belinda, and she suggested I see a psychiatric nurse practitioner who she worked with. She was not happy that I didn't disclose my bipolar disorder diagnosis, and she told me about it. But she did put me in contact with someone who could help. Because of the onset of flashbacks while in therapy with Belinda, I decided to take some time off from therapy, thinking maybe it was the actual therapy causing the flashbacks.

Now that I was back in my home, I would walk to the front of the house and look out the windows. Sometimes I saw a police car drive by, and when I saw them my head exploded with fear. The adrenaline shot through my system along with all the other stress hormones. It made me very nervous, and I felt like I was being targeted. Like they were lurking to see if I did something wrong so they could arrest me and throw me in jail.

I sat outside by the pool with Mom and Christy, and we came up with a plan for me to temporarily move up to the mountains and put the house on the market. I was so ready to be out of the house and away from all the reminders of my psychotic episode and everything which came with it. Just being in that environment alone added to my anxiety, even if I wasn't completely aware of it at the time.

I quickly got to work finding a place where I could feel safe, but it would still be close enough for me to get to the airport within a reasonable amount of time. I needed the proximity to the airport because I traveled weekly for work. I was still employed by a biotechnology company but had taken family medical leave.

Between the three of us, we found a beautiful three-bedroom log cabin in Payson, Arizona for rent. It was just under an hour and a half drive to Phoenix. Payson was almost five thousand feet in altitude, which would make the remainder of the summer much more tolerable as the temperature was far below the desert scorchers of 100-plus degrees.

I loved the idea of living in the mountains. For years, I had wanted to write a book. Like many people, my dream was to become a writer. I imagined having my sacred writing space in a log cabin with glass windows, backing up next to snow-capped mountains. But that was just a dream.

~

When the middle of July came around, it was time to leave my home in Phoenix. I quickly made arrangements for a moving company to come and pick up all of my furniture and belongings. I put the vast majority of my things in a storage unit, and the rest we moved into the rental property.

The cabin was set in a nice neighborhood and had a hot tub in the backyard. It also had a really cool wooden cabana space with a chair and table. Surrounded by nature, it was the perfect place to relax and try to regain my sanity.

In the cabin, the moment I set up my computer I made the decision to write a book. I had been writing in a journal for years and used writing as a way to express my feelings. It wasn't a huge leap for me to think I could write a book. When I graduated from college at the University of Arizona, I had a professor in a class called The Communication of Literature. I would walk with him across campus after class and listen to his philosophical views on life, literature, and relationships. He would always say when it came to fictional stories that there was a fine line between what is "true" and what is the "truth." This always struck me that sometimes in fictional writing an author can say much more than what we may say when writing non-fiction. I later would come to my own conclusion that writing non-fiction could still be very expressive, and I appreciated the ability to do some "truth telling."

As much as I had been through, I managed to create a fictional story called "Concealed Wounds." This artistic expression allowed me the opportunity to use my skills and imagination and freely express my thoughts and feelings. I also wrote several poems that I incorporated into the book.

I didn't really have any experience writing fictional stories, but I did come to learn I loved to tell stories. The opening scene begins with a woman, Norah, locked in a psychiatric hospital seclusion room crying out as she experiences flashbacks. Sound familiar?

I have to kind of chuckle because I made the two main characters' experiences similar to my own with big sprinkles of imagination. The exceptional psychologist sent to help the main character was completely fictional, except she had some experiences that were actually "true." Looking back, I believe I created this character as someone who I hoped would come into my life. Almost like manifesting or drawing toward me what I had wished for. A therapist who could understand me and care enough to gently help me through my trauma. It would take years for this person to appear in my life, but eventually she did.

I spent several weeks during that summer writing that book. It was a great escape from the harsh realities and additional trauma I had experienced. But it was the beginning of how I would use creativity as one of my go-to coping strategies in the next several years.

The cover I chose for the book was the classic case of *a picture says a thousand words*. I articulated my vision for the cover to a graphic designer, and she made it look exactly as I had imagined.

The cover had three silhouettes. One was a young girl with a baseball cap on backward. The second was a high school age girl standing straight forward. The last was an adult female with her arms behind her back. Each one of them was standing side-by-side in a field of sunflowers directly behind three tombstones. The sky in the background had some storm clouds, but a streak of bright orange light poked through the darkness. Between the sunflowers and the light, it represented my hope. The tombstones were a symbol of how trauma made me wish I could end my suffering. But the standing silhouettes were the triumphant reminder that I had won those battles. I had no idea what my life journey was going to look like, but I still had hope everything was going to be okay.

I knew the quality of my novel wasn't going to land me on a bestseller list. I decided the goal was to publish it quickly and put it in the hands of the people who supported me. I self-published the book and in the meantime learned a little bit more about the publishing industry, just in case I ever wrote another book.

When the printed books arrived, Christy and Mom were so excited for me. They loved reading each chapter as I finished the story. Of course, in their biased view, the book was awesome, but I knew it wasn't. It did, however, accomplish what I had set out to do. The level of focus it required to complete sentences and create a story kept my mind in the present moment. I didn't know it at the time, but I was processing the trauma caused from my psychotic episode and dealing with less than knowledgeable or compassionate police officers.

Jack, a friend of Mom's, read my book and began to relentlessly encourage me to continue writing. In the past, he worked for a newswire as a writer, so he had some credibility in my eyes. But my doubts had swarmed over me, and it would take almost ten years before I had enough confidence to write another book.

When I wasn't writing, I spent a great deal of my time with Chance, Shasta, and Buddy on the hiking trails. Hiking was a hobby of mine I'd done for many years. From the mountains in Colorado and Tennessee to the frequent hikes in the Grand Canyon, there wasn't anything I liked better than to find a peaceful place on a trail and start walking.

One of my favorite moments was to be still and watch my dogs run. Their eyes sparkled and their ears flopped as the freedom to roam provided incredible joy. Hiking was my spiritual sanctuary.

For the nearly ten years I lived in Phoenix, most often I could walk out my back door and land on a trail. In Payson, it was a ten-minute drive to a National Park Forest where trails were in abundance.

When I wasn't writing or hiking, sometimes Mom and I would go into town and find a unique spot to explore. One day we went into a bar and restaurant that had a piano. I approached the bartender and asked if I could come in and play sometime. She said, "Sure. No problem. We'd love to have you play."

She didn't know my repertoire of music wasn't really suited for a bar, as I played mostly love songs from the 70s, old hymns, and ballads from a *Reader's Digest* piano book. Most of the patrons paid no attention to the music in the background. I just went through the book page by page and played what songs I had mastered.

I had been playing the piano since I was six years old. The piano was a soothing outlet for me, especially because it required me to concentrate on what I was doing and not allow my mind to wander. It was a way of staying in the present moment before I ever knew anything about mindfulness. My sister Cindy and I would have marathon music sessions where we took turns playing the piano and singing. My music had been traveling with me as my life journey led me from one city to another. Even though I had a keyboard, I was always in search of a real piano where I could play.

Those positive memories really helped me as I struggled to find some semblance of normalcy. Playing the piano was another artistic expression that served as a coping strategy. And years later, the thought of me drinking a diet Coke and playing "The Impossible Dream" in a bar still makes me laugh.

~

As the weeks and months passed, I became stronger mentally and physically. I was struggling a bit with moderate depression, but I wasn't haunted by daily flashbacks, and I attribute that to taking a long break from therapy. In all honesty, I thought I functioned better without it. Years later, I would learn no therapy is far better than bad therapy.

After nearly three months of being off work, I went back in September 2006 for a biotechnology company. I started traveling by plane again, and soon after, the combination of stress and my underlying mental health conditions again triggered flashbacks. I remember taking a nearly two-hour flight from Phoenix to Denver. When I got on the plane, my chest was tightening. I went to the very back of the plane. I sat down and put my face in my hands. Tears, so many tears were leaking out my eyes. I was doing the kind of crying that made my stomach sick. Right before the plane started to take off, I began to shake. I knew a flashback was coming.

As soon as the plane was in the air, I went into the lavatory. I closed the lid to the toilet seat and sat down. My whole body began to tremble. It didn't help to try to fight it. I had to let it happen or run its course. I could feel pure terror. After I stopped shaking, I lifted my head and looked in the mirror. My eyes had a hollowed-out look, as if I'd seen a ghost. I was unrecognizable to myself. I was dressed like a businesswoman, but I felt like a child.

I stayed in the lavatory until we were preparing for landing in Denver.

No one said anything to me during the flight until the flight attendant knocked on the door and said, "Ma'am? Ma'am? Are you okay?"

"Yes, I'm okay. I'll be right out."

"It's time to take your seat," she said politely.

I exited the lavatory after splashing water on my face. My makeup was streaking down my cheeks and my face was blotchy. I glanced at the flight attendant as I went to sit down. She looked at me but didn't say anything. I could only imagine what she might have been thinking.

When the plane arrived at the gate, I took a deep breath and walked down the jetway. I started to sob. As I walked through the busy airport, the noise seemed thunderous to me. I found a shoeshine stand without anyone there and sat on one of the steps. I was trembling and couldn't hold back my tears. The flashbacks lasted no longer than a few minutes most of the time. However, the aftereffects could linger for hours. I had no choice but to pick myself up and forge onward. I had to work to support myself.

After sitting at the stand for a while, a young man came up to me and said, "I wish there was something I could do to take your tears away. I'm sorry you're sad."

I picked my head up and simply said, "Thank you."

He wished me well and walked away. The fact that someone stopped and showed a little compassion gave me the strength to get up and start walking to the rental car bus. I collected myself on the bus ride, got into my rental car, and headed to my hotel for the night.

Years later, I would find a passage in a well-known book about trauma. The author suggested that the actual trauma causing events, however horrendous, had a beginning, middle, and end. Flashbacks, on the other hand, were almost worse than the actual events because they often came out of nowhere and there was no way of knowing when they would stop. The flashbacks had a way of retraumatizing. They were relentless and painful.

Even though flashbacks have some psychotic symptoms, like hallucinations, they are not considered a psychotic episode. At the time, I was taking medications to help prevent a psychotic episode, and while in theory these medications may help flashbacks, they never prevented mine.

Because my mental health challenges were so significant, I made up my mind to move back east to be closer to my family so I could have their support as I struggled to function with daily activities and taking care of my dogs. I needed Mom and other members of my family's help. Even though I was functioning at work, I would often find myself on the verge of exhaustion. Going to the grocery store or cooking a meal was too difficult of a task. I could feed my dogs, but it was more helpful if my mother did it.

Anytime I had a break, I would lie in my bed with the covers tucked under my chin. The moment my body hit the bed, my three dogs—Shasta, Chance, and Buddy—would find their spot. Having them with me provided a tremendous amount of comfort. One of the worst remnants of my flashbacks was a lingering feeling of fear. My dogs helped put me at ease, and that ease gave me a slice of peacefulness.

It was evident to me, since I was alone, being closer to my family would provide a great deal of the help I needed. At the time, the biotechnology company I worked for didn't have any jobs in the area, so I began a job search online and found a medical device company with a job listing in the Pittsburgh area that was only an hour away from Mom's home in West Virginia. I sent my resume in, and within a few days had a call back that they were interested and wanted me to fly to Pittsburgh for an interview.

On a fall day in October 2006, I took an earlier morning flight, did the interview, and then powered through it all and took a red eye home. I made the drive back to Payson and waited to hear back from the company. I was attempting to put what happened that summer in the rearview mirror and try to move forward with my life.

The company didn't take long to notify me I'd gotten the job. Mom and I packed up my thirty-four-foot RV, all the dogs, and headed for West Virginia. The moving company took care of all the rest of my belongings. It was time to turn the page on my years in Arizona and start somewhere new. Four months had passed since I had my encounter with law enforcement. My hope was the move would be good for my mental health.

Before I left town, I saw Belinda one last time. We were discussing the psychotic episode I had in June, and she said to me, "You just get real crazy and freak out." I felt like she shamed me for what happened, and since I hadn't had a psychotic episode in six years and never had a flashback before in my life, I blamed her for what happened to me and questioned the effectiveness of her treatment methods, even though some part of me believed it wasn't her fault.

The psychiatric nurse practitioner I was seeing wrote prescriptions for the medications I was taking for ninety days. I thought I could find a psychiatrist before the prescriptions expired. Looking back, I was taking a major risk with my health in not having a more concrete plan to manage my mental health conditions. Without the proper medications, I was at risk for having another psychotic episode, and I now had proof when that happened it put my life in danger. But I didn't have those insights at the time. I rolled the dice and took my chances everything would work out.

Chapter 4

Mom and I finally made it to her house safely, after a more than a two-thousand-mile trek across the country. I was happy and relieved to be back in West Virginia with its rolling hills and winding roads. I had put a lot of distance between myself and my interaction with the police and the unpleasant memories unleashed on my soul in the Arizona desert.

I left my dogs with Mom and went to live in a temporary apartment in Pittsburgh, not far away from the medical device company office where I began working. It was a lot of change in a short period of time. Moving two times in less than a year is stressful enough, but adding a new job and two mental health conditions to the mix, and it's a recipe for challenging times ahead.

One of the first things I did when I started working was search the internet for a new psychiatrist. I found one north of Pittsburgh in an area where I had hoped to purchase a house. She said she specialized in PTSD and could take me as a new patient, but she couldn't see me for over three months. In the moment, I knew instantly I was going to run out of medications, but this psychiatrist seemed like a good fit. I kept the appointment and took my chances I'd be okay without a month or so of medications.

I felt like I was taking my mental health seriously, but as Mom always says, "If I knew then what I know now, things would be different." But hindsight is twenty-twenty. I didn't have the knowledge or experiences that I have today. But a lesson I learned the hard way is "there is no health without mental health." Something I wish I'd realized years ago.

Work at the medical device company was very stressful. I would find myself out walking the streets of Pittsburgh in the cold, dark evenings to try to manage the stress. I had only spent two years of my fifteen-year career in business behind a desk. In my first five years of working in the pharmaceutical industry, I worked in sales. Later I became a Regional and then National Account Director. I traveled frequently both by car and by plane. My work was predominantly with customers where having a home office allowed for greater flexibility than working a nine to five job.

The culture at the medical device company was very different from what I was accustomed to. People were nice, but not as willing to engage in social chit chat or collaboration. I had worked for a cutting-edge start-up pharmaceutical company that took the entire company to Pecos River, New Mexico for a few days of team building activities. Creativity, diverse thoughts, and contributions were encouraged. In that type of environment, I thrived. Every company I worked for after that experience, I had a difficult time adjusting. While most of the companies highly valued my creativity, their culture wasn't quite as progressive as the start-up pharmaceutical company.

At the medical device company, my office space was in a four-by-four cubicle in the back of the office building with limited windows. It was an effort to get to work every day. Wherever I turned, I was having to make some kind of adjustment. There were no more big blue skies and lots of sunshine. Pittsburgh was cloudy the vast majority of the year, and although there were plenty of hills, they weren't the mountains I was accustomed to seeing. At one point, I did some research and found Arizona had over three hundred days of sunshine a year, while Pittsburgh had around sixty-five. For a person like me who struggled badly with depression at times, the sunshine was a powerful antidote. But now I was going to have to make a monumental adjustment, to say the least.

After a couple of months, I found a three-bedroom house nestled into the western Pennsylvania woods on a large, private lot surrounded by massive oak trees. Living there gave me the opportunity to constantly reach out my door and touch some part of nature. Surprisingly to me, thirty minutes north of Pittsburgh guaranteed a whole lot more ice and snow. But despite the cold weather and lack of sunshine, it felt safe and peaceful to live among the many trees that welcomed squirrels, birds of many colors, and a playground for my three dogs. It was a home that reminded me of where I grew up, and that signified peacefulness to me, and though I had lived in several cities and suburbs, I felt most comfortable in a small town.

Moving into the house made my commute to work more difficult, but the company was building a new office about five miles from my new home. The new location would eliminate my constant daily struggle of sitting in a sea of cars as we all inched along toward our destinations. All I would have to do was stick it out until the company moved into the new location.

February 2007 came around, and the winter of snow, ice, and bitter cold was taking a toll on me. I was out of medications, even though the pharmacist suggested he call the nurse practitioner in Arizona to see if she would refill them for me. I remember walking back into the pharmacy and him telling me, "I'm sorry, Amy. When I ask her to refill your prescriptions, she said 'absolutely not!'" I told him not to worry. I had found a new doctor who could help me.

At the end of February, I eventually found my way to my new psychiatrist's office. Dr. Richard was on the second floor of a dated office building. There were two options to get upstairs—either take the elevator or climb the steep staircase. I opted for the latter.

Meeting Dr. Richard for the first time was rather unremarkable. She stood about 5'6" tall with heels, long, sandy colored hair pulled back, and a pair of square black glasses that frequently slid down her nose.

I let Dr. Richard know what happened in Arizona and when I started having flashbacks. She asked me several questions in our first meeting and then decided to prescribe an anti-depressant, indicating it would help with PTSD symptoms. Unlike in the situation with Belinda, I did disclose to Dr. Richard I had been diagnosed with bipolar disorder. I signed a release so she could obtain all my records from the other mental health professionals and hospitals I'd been to.

I don't really know if she ever read the records or not. She gave me different medications than the ones I had been taking when I left Arizona. I came to learn taking an anti-depressant when you have bipolar disorder can be risky. The anti-depressant can trigger mania. So, I'm not sure if she didn't think I had bipolar disorder or if she just took a risk on mania not being triggered. This was not a good way to start off with a new psychiatrist. Because I had waited so long to see her, I was very disappointed she didn't have a more comprehensive treatment strategy for me.

At my initial visit with Dr. Richard, she did recommend I begin seeing a therapist, Kendra, who worked with her in the office. I set up an appointment for the following week. Even though I had the experience with Belinda, which resulted in a not so good outcome for me, I didn't think to not trust Kendra. Maybe I was in such desperate need for help I gave every mental health professional the benefit of the doubt. At the time, all I had in my mind was to get on the right track, get mentally healthy, and move forward with my life. My hope was to leave the past behind me once and for all, and if a therapist could help me do this, I was all in.

Now that I've had years to sort out how bipolar disorder and PTSD affect me, I'm really uncertain as to why none of my psychiatrists ever simply said, "Maybe you have two mental health conditions. Both bipolar and PTSD." By 2007, there was a much greater amount of research on PTSD. There was also significant data on Adverse Childhood Events (ACES) which had been published in 1995 and 1996 by Kaiser Permanente. ACES shined a greater light on childhood trauma. A tremendous amount of research had been done on bipolar disorder, as well. The information would have been easily available to the mental health professionals who treated me. In fact, even the Diagnostic and Statistical Manual on Mental Disorders IV (DSM) alluded to the fact many people have co-occurring mood disorders with PTSD.

I find it hard to understand why the psychiatrists I saw didn't make it clear what my diagnosis was. Instead, they made it very frustrating and confusing. Even though I don't think it was intentional, it does demonstrate how difficult it is to get an accurate diagnosis.

After years of experience, I learned it is important to know what I was dealing with so I could attempt to make sense out of a very complex problem. I needed to understand symptoms and how they impacted me. It would take me years and much anguish to figure it out.

When I began seeing Dr. Richard, I continued my habit of writing in a journal. I was constantly attempting to make some sense out of what was happening to me by writing down various thoughts, feelings, and experiences. This was an entry from my journal in February 2007, and it sheds some light on how the flashbacks were affecting me:

"Dear friend, I woke up to a very beautiful day in my own home, my own bed, and my dogs surrounding me with love. By the way, sleeping in your own bed is important when you travel extensively for work. I stay in nice hotels, but they aren't like being home. Then, a flashback started again. My stomach is very sick. My head dizzy. My legs are chilled at this very moment. All was well this morning. I was sitting outside enjoying the sunny, warm, winter day opening my stack of mail after several days of being on the road for work. Symptoms: I feel like I'm going to throw up. The dizziness passes and then comes again. Chills. Pain. I know I can't be hurt now. I know where I am. I know I'm 42 years old. The breeze feels good brushing my face. But my hands are shaking. Sometimes my eyes can't focus, like I have blurred vision. I feel dirty. My ears feel dirty. My hair itches. My hand is icky and sticky. Is it the soda pop?"

Chapter 5

After a few months working for the medical device company, I simply could not endure the day-to-day office setting. Even the shorter commute was not going to make a difference. I started job searching and found an opportunity in the Pittsburgh area with the same biotechnology company I had worked with in Phoenix. Since I had left on good terms, they were willing to rehire me. I met with the regional director, and he offered me a position that would start in a few weeks.

I was so happy and relieved to be going back to a field position where I would have to travel to various locations around the east coast, but I would not have to work in a cubicle. The day-to-day office setting had never been something I enjoyed, and the cubicle made me feel like an animal trapped in a cage. Nor did it suit my need to move around and work off some of the anxiety I had to deal with. It was a good decision to return to the biotech company.

A few days after I received my offer letter, I pulled into the post office on a spring day in March 2007. It had been nine months since my encounter with law enforcement in Arizona. I remember the sun shining through the partly cloudy sky. I picked up the certified letter and walked back to my car. Sitting in the front seat, I looked at the envelope. It showed there were three attempts to deliver the notice to me. It indicated the certified letter had been forwarded from my two previous addresses in Arizona. On the outside of the envelope, I could see it was from a court in Phoenix.

I opened the letter, and as soon as I saw the first paragraph, my head began to spin. I started sobbing, shaking, my chest was tightening, and I was breathing rapidly. I was having a panic attack. The letter said I was being charged with two felony class 6 counts. The first was for assault against a peace officer, and the second charge was for resisting arrest. The date the charges were filed was December 25, 2006. Merry Christmas to me!

I had known I resisted getting into the back of the police car, but I couldn't figure out how I had assaulted the cop with sandy hair whose shoe was under my face. I never touched him. I don't know what Jan or the pool man witnessed, but I remembered most of what I did. My version of the story became a bit irrelevant, as I now had very little time before I had to appear in court in Arizona. I received the letter on March 2 and was supposed to appear in court on March 1, 2007. I didn't know how the court could hold me accountable to a date I didn't even know existed. I knew I needed an attorney as soon as possible.

Rushing home, I shared the devasting news with Mom, who had come up to help me with some home improvements, like painting a few rooms in my house. I was crying, and she was trying to comfort me. She said, "We'll get an attorney. Don't worry. They'll drop those charges. You were sick." I wasn't so sure it was going to be simple in any way, but it did give me a glimmer of hope.

The next few days, I went about trying to find a defense attorney in Phoenix. I called an old friend who was an attorney and asked her for some help. She said she'd get back to me on someone who may be able to help me. She also said, "Look on the bright side. It's only a class 6 felony. It could be a lot worse." What? I didn't have any idea what she was talking about. In my mind, it was a horrible situation. I was feeling so overwhelmed with stress. I know she didn't mean it in a bad way, but her comment really struck a nerve and gave me a sinking feeling in my stomach.

I let Dr. Richard and Kendra know what was going on. I had only been seeing Kendra for a few weeks before this happened, so she didn't know me very well. Neither Kendra nor the doctor had a reaction to what I perceived was tragic news, but they did encourage me that everything would be okay. "You were sick at the time," Kendra pointed out. I agreed but was still stuck on the whole idea that the cop said I assaulted him, when the closest I got to him was when his shoe was inches from my face.

My patience was running thin, and I was the only person who could handle the situation, so I got on the computer and searched for a defense attorney. I found one who seemed like she was well experienced. I made the phone call. I talked to Beth, the attorney who I ended up hiring. Beth told me I'd have to pay her $5000 to take the case. I called back later in the day and gave her office my credit card information. What would I do if I couldn't afford an attorney? I'd have to take my chances with a public defender, and while there are some exceptional ones, their caseloads tend to be very heavy.

Focusing on work seemed to help relieve the fixation on my past traumas, which helped minimize the flashbacks. I had so much stress and pressure on me, but I continued to move forward with transitioning to the biotechnology company. There were a few administrative things I'd have to do, including submitting for a background check, which had always been standard procedure prior to being hired. The whole idea of a background check made me nervous, not understanding how any of this worked, since I now found myself facing criminal charges. In my nearly sixteen years in corporate America, I never once had to worry about what was going to show up in my background. All of a sudden, I'd become a criminal without even knowing for sure what I had done to earn the title. I was now worried about losing my livelihood in addition to all the other stressors in my life. I just kicked into survivor mode.

I called Beth back within a couple of days, and she advised me to waive my first appearance and go directly to the next step in the process. She said I would only have to make one trip to Arizona, and I could do the hearing and sentencing all in one day. Beth told me, "The goal is to have the felonies reduced to a misdemeanor. With a misdemeanor, you don't lose any of your rights. You can just explain away the charges if you're ever asked." On one level, I was understanding what she was telling me. On another level, I was numb. How could this be happening to me? What kind of sentencing does she mean? This seemed so unfair and torturous.

The information was only half sinking into my brain. I was still having flashbacks, dealing with anxiety and depression, and in the middle of changing jobs. Now legal issues. I had no choice but to trust Beth was giving me the best legal counsel. I didn't know anything about the criminal justice system. I didn't even understand the process she was trying to explain to me.

~

A few weeks passed before it was time to take the over four-hour flight from Pittsburgh to Phoenix. My day in court was April 5, 2007. We flew out the night before I had to show up to face the charges against me. Mom accompanied me on the trip, and we stayed at an older but nice resort in South Phoenix. I remember calling an old friend when I got there and asked her to come to court with me. I had spoken to her on the phone a few times in the prior week, so she was aware of my situation and had written a letter on my behalf for the court.

Although she was polite about it, she said she didn't want to get involved. Maybe I was just asking too much. All I could think of was thank God for my mother.

Having a serious mental illness was tough enough. Dealing with the fallout of the consequences was like stabbing my heart with a knife. Not to mention the fact I didn't bring any of this on myself...or did I?

There was much blame to go around. The perpetrators who had made me a victim were nowhere in sight. The police and the court didn't even know I had PTSD and bipolar disorder. I didn't know what I had or what I didn't. Not even Beth asked me about my mental health conditions. What I did know is that I had a psychotic episode, and that made me a very vulnerable person. It put me in danger. Now I was paying a price for having an undertreated mental illness.

When I talked to Beth on the phone, she said she would meet us outside the court building in plenty of time to review the police report and talk about my options. I remember having a queasy feeling in my stomach as we approached the court building. The driver dropped us off, and we walked over to a cement outdoor table and bench and sat down. The sun beat down with an intensity that only happens in the desert.

Mom said in an encouraging way, "Everything is going to be alright. You'll see. Try not to worry too much."

I stared through her as I played my version of what happened on that June day in 2006 in my head, sometimes disconnected from my emotional self and other times overwhelmed.

The phone rang, and I answered.

"Amy, this is Beth. I'm calling to let you know I've gotten tied up with another case, so just go into the court building and I'll meet you there," she said, rushed.

"Okay. We'll find our way there," I said without any emotion.

I turned to my mother, repeated the conversation with Beth, and said, "Let's go and get this over with."

We walked toward the large court building, and my mind wandered to the two times I'd been there before. Once when I was summoned for jury duty, and the other time to watch a friend in action as she prosecuted a case. I never expected to find myself intersecting with the criminal justice system.

As we inched closer to the entrance, it felt more like a humbling walk of shame. The kind of shame that strips your confidence away. I put my personal belongings in a plastic dish as we walked through the metal detectors. I asked one of the security guards where the superior courtroom was, and he pointed us in the right direction. The section outside the courtroom consisted of several crowded benches. Mom and I had a difficult time finding a seat, and we kind of crowded our way into a small space and sat down. I glanced around and couldn't help but notice most people there weren't white females dressed in a business suit. I was in the minority and stood out like an unfortunate person caught in the wrong place at the wrong time. My stomach was in knots, and the sweat was dripping down my back, making my silk blouse cling to my skin.

Beth finally came out and handed me the police report. She said the best option was for me to take a plea deal, which would eliminate any felony charges and I would *only* have a misdemeanor on my record. I had less than five minutes to read the police report and make a life altering decision.

When Beth came back and asked me for my decision, I said, "The police report is wrong. I never slapped the police officer. He lied in multiple places on this report."

Beth answered, "It's your word against his, and who would believe you given your state of mind? Your best option is to take a plea deal. Otherwise, you'll have to make several trips back to Arizona for trial, and if you lose, you'll go to jail. You don't want that, do you?"

Of course, I didn't want to go to jail. I just couldn't get over the fact he lied on the report. He even said I called myself the devil and was chanting. In the psychotic episodes I'd had, I've never once called myself the devil. Angel maybe, but devil...no way. And as far as chanting, no. Singing spiritual songs at the top of my lungs, yes. Part of what has made my journey so difficult is I remember a great deal of what has happened during psychotic episodes. It's not pleasant to remember what I did when I was out of touch with reality. I've had to overcome a great deal of shame because of it.

But who would believe me that I remembered what happened? Why would the cop do something like this? What had I done that was so horrible he would make up an assault charge? I'd never been violent a day in my life. Even in my compromised mental health states, I was never violent. And then I replayed that day in my mind. I did push the Marine. I was trying to pull Jan in the pool. I would later find out neither of them wanted to press charges. But I never once slapped or hit that cop with an open left hand, as he said I did in the police report. If I was going to slap someone, I'd hit them with my dominant hand, and that would be my *right hand*.

Sitting outside the courtroom, I was overwhelmed with humiliation. My resistance didn't last long, as I agreed to take Beth's counsel and took a plea bargain agreement. I pleaded "no contest" because I wasn't going to admit I did something I did not do, and that was a moral victory. However, the court records reflected a guilty plea. The next step was to wait until they called my name in court. Beth told me if I wanted to say something to the judge, I would have my opportunity in the courtroom. My mind was racing. I couldn't link a coherent sentence together if my life depended on it. Everything was happening so fast.

Beth, Mom, and I walked into the courtroom. Beth stood on my left side, and Mom stood behind us. We were positioned in about the middle of the small courtroom behind a tall table with a microphone attached. I don't remember Beth saying anything to me. She could have, but I was numb and emotionless.

Somehow, I managed to keep my head up and look at the judge, when all I wanted to do was crawl under something and hide or maybe disappear altogether.

The judge read the charges against me and asked me how I'd like to plead. I said, "No contest." He asked me if I'd like to say anything. I leaned forward, pulled the microphone toward me, and then shook my head. He sentenced me to one year probation, court ordered counseling, no drinking any alcohol, and no contact with the cop. Because I had relocated to Pennsylvania, the court granted me an interstate compact, which allowed me to be supervised by the Pennsylvania probation officers.

Directly after court, Mom and I made our way over to the Phoenix probation department. It was swarming with people. I got to the counter and was given my instructions. I've rarely ever felt total defeat in my life, but in that moment in the probation office in Phoenix, I was despondent, devastated, and defeated. How could I have let this happen to me?

~

After receiving all my probation instructions, my mom and I rushed to the airport to take our flight home. When the plane took off from the Phoenix airport, I couldn't have been more relieved. As much as I loved Arizona, I couldn't care less if I ever stepped foot there again. All the good memories I had made there disappeared from the forefront of my mind. I had a bad taste in my mouth, and it was going to take years for it to dissipate.

We made it back to Pennsylvania, and shortly thereafter I started inquiring with the biotechnology company when my official start day would be. I was told there would be slight delay until they verified some additional information. I had already left my job with the medical device company, had purchased a new home, and incurred plenty of expenses in our Phoenix excursion. Not having a job was not an option.

Fortunately, human resources called me and let me know when they did the background check it came back with one word, "convicted." They talked it over with the CEO of the company.

The HR person said to me, "Seth says he understands this is probably something that happened while you were in Arizona. He's going to overlook this, but he wants you to know if it ever happens again, you'll be fired."

There's no doubt I felt uncomfortable and insecure with Seth's comment. I knew from my mother's experience with bipolar, episodes were part of the illness. I didn't yet understand how most of the episodes could be avoided with the proper treatment. I was already very insecure about others knowing I struggled with mental illness. His comments added to that insecurity. But I was relieved Seth was willing to overlook what happened in Arizona, and I appreciated the second chance.

I hung up the phone and danced around the house with my dogs. I yelled out several "thank Gods." I had gotten a needed break.

I called Mom and let her know the good news. She said, "You've got a bunch of guardian angels looking out for you." It sure felt that way.

Chapter 6

Sometimes I seemed to be a very lucky person, and other times it felt like I couldn't catch a break. After working full-time for a biotech company, while serving out my one-year probation sentence, the impact of the 2008 financial crisis had a direct effect on my working environment. The small biotech company, like many other companies, laid off over ninety percent of their employees in February that year. I was one of the lucky ones they kept. Even with my mental health difficulties, I was a very high performing employee. But this meant myself and one of my colleagues who worked in reimbursement would have to split the country and service our customers. This would mean extensive cross-country trips for me. I had previously worked in the western U.S., and because of that I inherited the west coast after the layoffs.

This was an enormous amount of stress on my body and mental health. Flying across the country meant frequent time zone changes, and that would interrupt my sleeping patterns, and the pace of this type of lifestyle was anxiety-ridden. I would rush from the airport to my hotel room, completely amped up. At times I had intrusive memories about the sexual abuse I was processing in therapy, and that would add to my anxiety. I was never actively trying to think about the traumatic events, they would simply show up in either memories or flashbacks. I had many triggers that would start the domino effect. A trigger could be as simple of a phrase such as, "Just checking." Anytime I heard that phrase, I was transferred back in time to a very dark place, and it felt like the trauma was happening all over again. I hadn't yet learned how to preemptively identify a trigger, let alone process the emotions from the memory. On one hand, I was the adult businesswoman flying first class, and on the other hand, I felt like a child continuously living a real live nightmare.

From the time I started sexual abuse therapy in 2005 with Belinda in Arizona, until I had been seeing Kendra for over a year, even though I struggled, somehow, I managed to pick myself back up and keep on fighting. But flashbacks put my body in a continued state of arousal. The fight-flight stress response was on overdrive, constantly pouring adrenaline and cortisol into my system. During a flashback, I would dissociate or get numb emotionally, leaving my body, reliving traumatic events. When it was over, I still had to deal with what I saw, tasted, heard, smelled, or felt during a flashback. By the end of my probation period in March 2008, I was hanging on by a thread.

As I thought about taking time off from work, I realized I hadn't been the most frugal person in my life, and the constant threat of losing my livelihood caused a lot of distress. I had ruminating thoughts about how difficult it would be for me to find another job because of the financial crisis and that rumination wasn't because I wouldn't have a good resume. It was because of a criminal record. I also had in the back of my mind the comments from the biotech CEO who said if I was sick again, like I was in Arizona, I would be fired.

Even though I had a misdemeanor, it was going to show up on background checks. Beth told me I could "explain it away." But the nature of the charge made it sound like I was a violent person, and that was very far from the truth. What I would come to learn was the sentence of one-year probation was more like a life sentence of being marked with a criminal charge. I was frustrated, disappointed, and questioning whether I had good legal counsel. I was obsessed because I felt as if I didn't deserve the charge or punishment.

I could hear Beth saying, "If you have a misdemeanor, you can explain away the charges. It won't matter to employers."

I said, "But it's the nature of the charge I'm worried about."

"You worry too much, Amy. It's only a misdemeanor." Beth reinforced her position.

"I realize I worry too much, but that doesn't mean this charge won't be an issue in finding a new job if I need to," I said, not understanding why Beth didn't see my point.

I would run through the conversations with Beth over and over in my head. At the time, I just couldn't let it go.

After years of sorting through all my varying emotions, I concluded I'll never know if there could have been a different outcome. The only other option would have been going to trial, and knowing what I know now, I doubt a person with mental illness would have been shown understanding and compassion from a jury. It's basically a person with mental illness's word against a cop. Who's the jury going to believe?

Psychosis and flashbacks are complicated to explain, much less come to an understanding of how someone can remember so much detail after a psychotic episode. I figured there was no way anyone would believe I never slapped the cop. The only saving grace for me was that I knew I didn't do it. I could tell them what I did do; why wouldn't I be able to remember what I didn't do?

Time was marching on with or without my ability to accept my new reality. When I was finally discharged from probation in March, it was like releasing a pressure valve in my brain. While they allowed me to travel for my work, when I was home, I could only go five miles away, which was about enough to go to the grocery store. This meant I would only take two ninety-mile trips to West Virginia to see my family in an entire year. Normally, I would have visited at the very least monthly, and always on every holiday. When I did travel to West Virginia, I had to have a permission slip signed by my probation officer to make the trip. Even though Mom and my niece Natalie visited, I was very isolated. If it wasn't for Chance, Shasta, and Buddy, life would have been pretty miserable.

By the time May arrived, I had been seeing Kendra for therapy and Dr. Richard for medication management for over a year. My mental health status wasn't getting better under their care. It was getting worse. I don't know if I expected the flashbacks to have ended, but I didn't expect them to happen more frequently.

I had monthly appointments with Dr. Richard. One day as I walked back to Dr. Richard's office, I could feel my chest tighten. I sat in the chair in front of her and began to shake and tremble.

She looked at me, shocked, and was startled so much she jumped back in her chair.

I said to Dr. Richard, "This is what is happening to me every day."

She answered, "I'm sorry, Amy. Isn't the medication helping you?"

"I don't know if it's helping. I just can't stop the flashbacks. I've been having them for more than a year now. As soon as I started therapy for sexual abuse," I said despondently, as if saying it was acknowledging how long I'd been dealing with them.

"Well, keep working with Kendra. She can help you with that."

And just like that, the conversation was over. No explanation. I just don't think she knew how to treat me. Retrospectively, I learned treating flashbacks is extremely difficult, even for psychiatrists who specialize in treating trauma patients. Dr. Richard's specialty was Child and General Psychiatry. She probably should have referred me to someone who specialized in treating trauma or at least to someone else who had more experience with trauma than she did.

One big issue I came to realize about ten years later was having the right diagnoses was important not only for me to know what symptoms to look out for so I could manage them, but also the right diagnoses were important for the treatment strategy.

While I was still very frustrated with all the psychiatrists I had seen up until that point, I have come to learn it is very difficult to differentiate a diagnosis. Especially when it comes to PTSD and other co-occurring disorders. There is scientific literature and there are studies, but there are many differences in opinions. Building consensus in mental health treatment is far more difficult than it is in medicine. Without definitive diagnostic tools, like MRIs, CAT scans, X-rays, and blood tests, it's far more difficult to gain agreement on what a diagnosis is and what treatments work best.

There are also competing interest groups who rail against pharmaceuticals and an entire movement on anti-psychiatry. Finding one's way through a maze of competing viewpoints is not an easy task. Before I worked for the biotech company, I had worked in the pharmaceutical industry. One benefit I had was selling or marketing products used for conditions like bipolar disorder, schizophrenia, and psychosis. I had many hours of training and interactions with psychiatrists at various medical facilities I called on as an account manager. I had enough background knowledge to make myself a much more informed consumer. But even with all this knowledge, it was hard to objectively apply it to my own situation—not impossible, just very difficult. It was difficult to be my own advocate, but something I would learn how to do in time.

As much as I believed in medication management when appropriate for mental health conditions, I also believed in therapy. I just couldn't find the right therapist to help me.

Like Belinda, Kendra seemed to be driven a great deal out of curiosity rather than therapeutically. In fairness, I was presenting with symptoms of PTSD, yet the flashbacks and intrusive memories were mostly from childhood. I would come to learn I had delayed expression PTSD, which is the exception rather than the rule. In other words, most people who develop PTSD develop it within six months after the traumatic event. Having such a late onset adds to the layers of complexity, and it's possibly why an earlier diagnosis in my journey with the mental health treatment system could have been missed.

I can say I learned quite a few things from Kendra that helped me deal with the aftermath of flashbacks. In one therapy appointment, Kendra explained a few coping strategies.

"Amy, the most important thing you can tell yourself is to stay in the present moment," Kendra said emphatically, continuing to harp on this to the point where I found it annoying.

"So, I just tell myself to stay in the present moment?" I asked, not sure what she meant at the time.

"Yes, focus on the five senses. It will ground you in the present moment and help you manage the flashbacks," Kendra said. "You can also tell yourself nothing bad is happening now."

"I think I understand," I replied, although I thought this sounded a lot simpler than it would be to actually follow through and do it.

"If you need to ground yourself, go to the mirror and repeat your name and age. This will also help bring you back into the present moment."

"I've been doing that grounding technique in the mirror for

months now. I saw it in a book I'm reading. Good to know I've been doing something right," I said with a little confidence.

The coping strategies were helpful after a flashback occurred, but nothing seemed to stop them. My attempt to stay in the present moment took a great deal of effort, but I wasn't always successful. One day I was working, driving along the Pennsylvania turnpike on narrow roads with tight cement block partitions. I was innocently daydreaming and not thinking about too much of anything, when suddenly I scrunched up my face, squinted my eyes, and began quivering. I was so afraid I was going to wreck the car I quickly got off an exit and pulled into a parking spot. I sat in the car shaking my head, as if to get rid of the traumatic memory.

On that day, I was taken back to my grandfather's basement where an incident of sexual abuse had occurred by my cousin, Joe. I could smell the mildew, even though there was no mildew in sight. I dry heaved so much my stomach hurt. I sat for as long as it took to collect myself, then I found a restroom, washed my face, and got back on the road to get to my customer appointment.

It helped I spent most of my life blocking out events, suppressing memories, or shutting out background noise. Even my sports background helped. I remember standing at the free-throw line in Connecticut with a stadium filled with over ten thousand people cheering for their home team. The crowd was yelling, "Miss it," while I stood at the free-throw line. I had to block out the noise and focus on putting the ball in the basket. These things came in handy when I had to compartmentalize the aftermath of a flashback.

But that time in my life was no game. The skills to compartmentalize were crucial. After two years of having flashbacks, I had a method to cope and move on, and that was it. So far, the therapy did nothing to help with the flashbacks. Sometimes I think therapy made them worse. However, the flashbacks wore me down. I estimated I had over one hundred flashbacks from 2005 when I initially started therapy with Belinda, until 2008 while I was in therapy with Kendra.

Adding to that was off the charts stress from probation, workplace stress, and the drain of mental health challenges. I went to Kendra in May, and during one of my appointments asked her if she thought it was a good idea for me to take time off work.

"You know, every person has her breaking point," I said to Kendra. "Would you support me in taking time off work to deal with these issues? I'm so exhausted I don't think I can take any more. I'd like to take short-term disability."

"Yes, I will support you," Kendra said quickly. "Tell me what you need from us, and Dr. Richard and I will do the paperwork for you."

In a less than five-minute conversation, the trajectory of my life changed dramatically. I had been earning a high level of income for a few years and geared my lifestyle to reflect it. I was hoping to take short-term disability and return to work within three months. I never thought about the current work environment or the economic recession. I just threw up a white towel and surrendered. It was the only solution I thought I had. If I could focus intensely on healing, perhaps I could get better faster. I couldn't go on any longer with violent flashbacks interrupting my days and turning my nights into terror.

At the same time, not working meant I no longer had a distraction to focus my mind on besides the traumatic events that were coming up. While it was beyond difficult to work while I was struggling with my mental health, it still provided me with a healthy coping outlet. When that outlet went away, my mental health declined significantly.

When I took my leave from work in May, I also went to two days a week for therapy with Kendra. In retrospect, two days a week therapy was far too intense, and I think it really messed me up by flooding myself with one traumatic memory after another. Only years later when I learned about trauma-informed care did I realize it may not have been a healthy or safe approach to trauma therapy to overwhelm my system by rehashing the contents of my flashbacks and the intrusive memories haunting me. I could only process so many emotions, feelings, and thoughts at one time. Kendra was indirectly asking me to process years of trauma from one appointment to the next, taxing my system and putting my emotions on overdrive. The therapy itself was triggering.

In 2020, during the pandemic, I learned from reading *The Body Keeps the Score* that "reliving the trauma repeatedly in therapy may reinforce preoccupation and fixation." While for years I had an intuitive feeling the sexual abuse therapy with Belinda and the trauma therapy with Kendra had contributed to the declining mental health I experienced, it wasn't until I read the book that I felt vindicated and equally sorry for the many women and men who unknowingly may experience something similar in therapy as I did. I wanted to get better with therapy, not worse.

At the very least, Belinda and Kendra should have given me a fair warning that trauma therapy can be very triggering. I don't know if knowing how intense the therapy could be would have mattered, but it certainly would have been the right thing to do to explain what can happen with trauma therapy. With additional information, at least I could have made the decision whether or not it was the kind of therapy that was going to work for me at that time in my life.

Chapter 7

In May 2008, the day after I took my leave from work, I went to the local Best Buy and purchased a video camera, screenwriter software, and a Mac computer. I had a vision to create a screenplay for a movie based on what I was experiencing. Most days, I couldn't concentrate enough to journal or write, so I figured I'd try my hand with technology for some kind of creation.

When I first began using the camera, one of the very first videos I shot I'm talking to Kendra. I wanted to show her my backyard. I remember taking the camera in to show her the footage. She was impressed with the large backyard and made a comment about my tractor, which seemed to embarrass me. I don't remember what she said, I only remember how I felt. While she was watching the video I made for her, I turned off the camera within the first couple of minutes. Maybe I just wasn't ready for anyone outside my family to know I owned a tractor, or maybe I didn't want her to see what I was doing in my backyard. I'm really not sure.

I purchased the tractor during the summer of 2007. My property was just under two acres, and while part of it was fenced in for the dogs, the house and property were in the woods. While I was on probation and couldn't leave my home, I took the time to create a nature trail. I cleared all the dead trees and chopped up the wood with a chainsaw I purchased and taught myself how to use. The trail weaved in switchback fashion from the edge of the fence in my backyard to a narrow creek. The tall oak trees were so close together the sunshine couldn't slip through even a crack during the summer. The dogs and I spent every day when it wasn't raining walking the trail, especially during the time I was on probation. The outdoors and nature had always been a safe sanctuary for me. Between my backyard and the nature trail, I had everything I needed to keep myself safe, and that is one of the things Kendra stressed to me. When each therapy visit was about finished, she would say, "Remember to keep yourself safe, Amy." I'd nod in acknowledgement and walk out the door.

By spring 2008, even though I was no longer on probation and could technically go anywhere I wanted, the backyard was a place where I felt completely safe. The tractor became something I used on my family's farm in West Virginia when I could travel there. I would put it on the back of a trailer and take it with me when I went to Mom's for a visit. I worked on another small trail in the woods on the vast acreage of land my family collectively owned. The woods were great as long as they didn't get overgrown with briar bushes and trees crowding each other out for the sunshine, but it took a lot of work and time to maintain it.

Growing up on a farm, I remember as a child how the tractor represented something that I frequently played on. When I think back, I can see myself walking across the lane over to the hayfield where the tractor sat. As young as four years old, I would climb up the back of the tractor and hoist myself onto the old, rusty seat. With my short blonde hair blowing in the wind, stuffed toy on my lap, I'd sit for as long as my mother would allow me to play on that tractor. It was total bliss to have such a wide-open space where I could pretend and play without any interruption or teasing from my older siblings.

For several years, my dad would let me sit on his lap while he drove the tractor down the road and into a barn for storage. As I grew older, he would let me steer. And then the day came when out of necessity I got to drive the tractor by myself. The old, red, slightly rusted Farmall tractor was like a safe and peaceful private playground for me. It was quite different from the modern, easy to drive, orange Kubota tractor I purchased in 2007.

My first experience of actually driving the tractor came during a sunny day in the spring, and it was potato planting time. My father used a hand plow that was attached to the back of the tractor to plow the dirt into rows. He had to stand behind the tractor with the plow attached, while my job was to drive the tractor in a straight line and keep the front left wheel on the upper side of the row. He would coach me by saying, "Keep it straight. Give it some gas. That a girl!" One of my fondest memories of my father was all the "that a girls" he gave me, and the day he let me operate the tractor, I was only nine years old.

For as long as I can remember, I always wanted to be with my dad. It seemed like he was always doing the kinds of things I enjoyed, like fishing, being outside in the woods, taking care of cows, and especially using the tractor. Inside the house, I was one of five kids, but outside with my dad, I was like an only child. Being with my dad and playing on the tractor was a safe place, peaceful and fun. I only wonder if my subconscious mind knew I needed a safe place to "play."

~

From the very beginning of my video making, I believed I was going to recover, though honestly there were times I had doubts I could make it another day. I did believe absolutely that I was not alone. I had read stories about other survivors and saw the statistics about sexual abuse and assault. I knew at the time how common it was.

I wasn't going to let my voice be silenced. I knew on some level what I was experiencing was not as much out of the ordinary as I initially thought. I knew the people who had hurt me badly enough to contribute to causing PTSD would never be held accountable. I wasn't recording my journey for the guilty. I was recording my journey for survivors. In one of the first video segments I recorded, I said, "My name is Amy Jean Gamble, and I will speak my truth." That was my intention.

After the first day of shooting the clip for Kendra, I gathered up a few large stuffed animals the dogs liked to play with. I placed the black stuffed dog who represented my black lab, Chance, on one lounge chair, and a white stuffed rabbit with big floppy ears on the other lounge chair. I began filming my first scene of "If the Toys Could Talk," saying "action" into the camera.

In a Chance character voice, I began talking. "Hi, my name is Chance, and I'm here to be your narrator, and I'm going to tell you a story. A story about which you probably know pieces…"

"Oh, no…oh, no," I say as my yellow Labrador, Shasta, runs onto the lounge chair and grabs the stuffed dog in her mouth.

I start laughing and then say, "Cut!"

I continue filming, and in my own voice say, "Oh, boy, everybody came to the party. We have some cutting footage here," followed by more laughing, as Chance and Buddy the beagle join in to play with Shasta.

"Let me have the dog, Shasta." I continued laughing. "Okay, let me have the main character—okay, okay, you can play with the main character. I'll have to find a different main character. Okay. Who gets to tell the story? Who wants to tell the story?"

I focus the camera on the other lounge chair where I had placed the white rabbit, and in a character voice, I say, "I do…I do…"

In my own voice, I say, "Rabbie—Rabbie, have you found your voice?"

Rabbie answers, "I think so, Amy. I think I'm finding it. But I think it would be good for me—I think Rabbie should be the main character, Amy."

In my voice, "Do you want to—do you want to be the main character, Rabbie?"

Rabbie answers, "Yeah—cuz I was kinda the one you cried to."

"Okay. Rabbie, you'll be the main character."

Rabbie became the main character, which was the narrator for telling my story. One of her first lines is, "If toys could talk, then the world would be a better place. So, come along with me. I'll be your narrator for the story. It's okay. I can tell you it turned out okay. I'm tellin' you if toys could talk, then the world would be a better place. If you just paid attention to them, they really do talk, you know? Maybe not with voices, but with signs and symbols and all sorts of things. The real Rabbie…I'm actually a stand-in because the real Rabbie met her demise."

The real Rabbie was in a closet at my mother's house well into my adulthood. My mom said, "I just don't have the heart to throw her out." Everyone knew how important Rabbie was to me as a child. Finally, when I was at my mother's house for a visit, I suggested she "let go" of Rabbie. At that point, Rabbie became a dog toy for my dogs until she had no more stuffing left. She had served an incredible purpose during the course of her existence.

Rabbie first came to life when I was seven years old and my sister, Shelley, bought me a white stuffed bunny rabbit. She gave her to me for Easter. Rabbie knew all my secrets, as I talked to her every night during bedtime. Between my prayers and talking to Rabbie, I was articulating the traumas affecting me.

In addition to talking to Rabbie, I also talked to my imaginary friend named Deter. My mom would come into the bedroom and say, "Amy, who are you talking to?"

"Deter," I would answer, as I happily played by myself with my toys and books.

My older sister Shelley would sneak up on me and laugh hysterically as I talked openly to my imaginary friend. This imagination carried over to giving my toys different voices and letting them have conversations with one another. As much as I had bad things happen to me in my childhood, I had many coping strategies, and one of them was always leaning on my ability to imagine.

When I wasn't alone, I was often playing with my cousin, Rhonda, who was only a year younger than me. We got along really well. She lived on a farm and had lots of dogs, cats, and horses. I would go spend time at her house, and we would play for hours with a wide variety of living animals and toys. One of our favorite games was pretending we were cats and dogs. I think my desire to have my own dogs as I grew up came from the loving way Uncle Rick and Aunt Janie cared for their pets. The pets were part of the family. When I was an adult, that's how my dogs were treated, too. They were my kids, and I talked to them all the time.

The only dark memory about going to Rhonda's house was when I was six years old. That was the place where my first clear memory of my cousin, Joe, sexually abusing me occurred.

I remember climbing on the back of his dirt bike, putting my arms around his waist, and hanging on, while he sped down the road to a park the city was building on farmland. I loved feeling the breeze touch my cheeks as the bike picked up a little bit of speed. I was fascinated with the motor sound; it was as if it was relaxing to me. Then, the motor stopped and Joe took my hand, leading me toward a picnic shelter that was under construction. I remember him sitting me down in a pile of clumpy dirt.

This was my first clear memory of childhood sexual abuse. It's not surprising why I would have flashbacks about dirt. I don't have a distinct memory of enduring any type of sexual abuse prior to six years old. However, in my healing journey, I did have countless reoccurring flashbacks of my stays with Joe's mom.

I was an easy target for Joe. My mother went to work when I was three years old. Most often she would work in the evenings, which would mean I'd be safe at home with my sisters and dad. I was almost four years old when she changed her shift and started working during the day, and I would often end up at Joe's house where his mom would take care of me, or at my grandfather's house where Joe would visit frequently. I didn't like going to Joe's house. Looking back, I'd say it was most likely because it was a tumultuous environment. After his mother died, Joe had lived for a few years with my mother's brother, Uncle Rick, and his family.

~

Nine. Nine was my magical number. Not only did I start driving the tractor, I began to stand up for myself. At nine, I wrote a very explicit letter to my mother telling her about how my cousin, Joe, who was almost twenty-one, had been sexually abusing me. I used a wide ruled piece of paper from a school notebook and a number two pencil. In sloppy cursive writing, I started the letter with "Dear Mommy…" One line from the letter said, "This has got to stop," indicating to me even as young as I was, I somehow knew how wrong what was happening to me was. Although I didn't have words to describe it as "sexual abuse," I could describe the acts, and Joe's acts were escalating to a point where I felt the terror in the moment while it was happening. I'd never been so afraid before that moment.

Holding Rabbie by one ear and with the letter rolled up into a square in my other hand, I jumped out of bed. My bare feet hit the cold hardwood floor, and I went to find my mother. I gave her the letter and ran back to my room and got under the covers, clinging to Rabbie and whispering in her tear-matted fur ear, not quite sure of the response I was going to get.

My mother read the letter and came back into my room. She

gave me a big hug and said, "Everything is going to be all right. No one is going to hurt you anymore." She immediately went out to the living room and made a phone call to her brother, my Uncle Rick, demanding he have a conversation with Joe. I lay in my bed listening intensely to the conversation. I could only hear bits and pieces of what my mother said, but one thing I knew for sure was that she believed me, and that alone gave me a sense of relief.

Writing the letter and giving it to my mom put an end to Joe's abuse. I don't remember how many times Joe had abused me. All I can remember is feeling relieved I had told my mother. On some level, I knew what was happening to me was wrong, but I didn't understand the gravity of the effects until I became an adult.

At nine years old, I was using writing as a way to express myself and tell my mother in story form what had been happening to me. There's something about putting words down on paper that sometimes seems much safer than saying them out loud. It's surprising to me I figured this out in third grade, at nine years old.

A short time after I wrote the letter to my mother, I received a letter from Joe apologizing for what he had done. My mother stood in the doorway while I sat on the edge of the bed in my mother's room and saw my reflection looking back at me in the large bedroom mirror. I was nervous when she said she wanted me to read the letter. My stomach started aching with a churning, burning sensation that would come and go and last for years.

After reading the letter, my mother said, "Now it's time to put this behind you and move forward. Put the bad memories on the backburner." I nodded and understood that when bad things happened, I was supposed to block it out and keep going. While my mother gave me the letter I wrote her, I never saw the letter from Joe again.

When I look back in time, on one hand, I would say it was a really good philosophy of "get knocked down, get back up again and put the past behind you." On the other hand, it wasn't like I just got a bad grade in school and needed to bounce back from a small setback. While an overarching attitude of toughness served me very well over the years, I also had to learn the difference between emotionally burying problems and giving myself permission to realistically acknowledge and not minimize the sad parts of my history. I had to find the balance between letting go of the past and not dismissing my younger self's pain.

At nine, I also played on my first organized sports team—fast pitch softball. When my dad would get home from work and change his clothes, that was my cue to start asking him to play ball.

I would say, "Daddy, will you play catch with me?"

He would kind of chuckle and give a little pause before saying, "Go get the gloves and ball."

He would throw the ball to me and jokingly call me butterfingers when I missed and say, "Keep your eye on the ball." We played in the backyard so much I can't recall how often.

In school, I was taller than almost everyone in my class. I was for sure the tallest girl for most of elementary school. That meant I always stood out. I was always different, never really fitting in with groups of girls who didn't like sports, or boys who picked me as the only girl to play with them on the playground.

I got my sports start in softball and enjoyed playing that for six years. But my real passion was playing basketball. My dad bought me a basketball for Christmas when I was eleven years old. Basketball was one of the sports I'd been playing on the court with the boys during recess. I'd take my basketball and go to the basement and practice dribbling. My dad would sit near his workbench and tinker with various projects, while keeping one eye on my developing ball handling skills. He would say, "Get your head up. Don't look at the ball." When the weather was nice, I moved my practice to the driveway. I taught myself how to dribble between my legs and behind my back, something girls just didn't do very often back then. When I had that ball in my hand, nothing else mattered. I was locked in on bouncing it until my mother would call for me to come in the house.

While I was on a sports stage and was developing a persona of toughness, I was privately a highly sensitive kid who was holding on to secrets and learning quickly how to suppress my memories of sexual abuse. But the one thing I could trust to help me was my imagination.

In fourth grade, it helped me to learn I wasn't alone, when Sally, a classmate of mine, revealed to us how her Uncle Trent was sexually abusing her. I remember feeling my throat tighten and my stomach gnawing as Sally painstakingly told us in detail all about her encounters with her Uncle Trent. Of course, I was reminded of Joe and didn't feel so alone when she shared her story, but I was so afraid other kids in class would know my secret. I suggested Sally tell her mother. She said, "I did. She won't believe me." In my mind, I felt lucky and relieved my mother had believed me, even though I understood I had to hold the secret of sexual abuse.

I went home from school that day with two stick figures I had drawn on a piece of paper with the names of Sally and Uncle Trent under each figure. I connected their mouths and their lower half together with lines I had drawn on the paper. I didn't intend for anyone to find my paper, but it fell out of my backpack on the floor, and my mother saw it.

She creased her brow and said, "Let me have that paper, right now!"

I clenched my fist around it and refused to give it to her, until finally I relented and opened my hand.

She looked at me with disapproval and asked, "Is that issue we talked about still bothering you?" She asked in a way that was not really welcoming me, to be honest.

"No!" I replied and shook my head rapidly.

"Well, if it is, I'll take you to the mental health center!" she said in a very stern way, as if I had done something wrong.

At ten years old, during the encounter with my mother, my father heard the slight commotion and called to me to come with him to feed the cows. "Amy, come on, let's go," my father called from the basement. I grabbed my coat and ran down the stairs, relieved to be going outdoors in the brisk cold and taking care of the cows, while sliding tears down my face helped me to cope in that moment. The level of stress I felt got bottled up inside of me and temporarily released into the outdoors, where I felt safe with my father.

I'd gotten the message loud and clear that I needed to keep the issue of sexual abuse to myself and one way or another figure out how to deal with it on my own. It was a strong message of the necessity for me to isolate myself and not bring up issues or problems. This would prove to have a tremendous effect on my life as an adult. Subsequently, that was the last time I ever mentioned to my mother the sexual abuse by Joe, until over thirty years later in the summer of 2008.

When I was at my grandfather's house, Joe and I made my first trip to Mr. Brock's store where Joe bought me candy and soda. Two years after I wrote the letter to my mother, when I was in fifth grade, I wandered into Mr. Brock's store on my own. He lured me behind the counter and told me to fill up a bag of candy. Then he grabbed me, restraining me from moving and placing me on his lap. I could see his brown-haired granddaughter who was a toddler come running behind the counter, as Mr. Brock shouted, "Get out of here!" But I was able to get out of his grip, and Mr. Brock was forced to stop his despicable act.

I grabbed the bag of candy and ran all the way back to my grandfather's house, which was a few blocks away. I was in fifth grade when that happened. I never went back to Mr. Brock's store again, but I carried the traumatic experience with me years later and all the way to Arizona, when the cop's shoe reminded me of Mr. Brock's shoes.

~

While basketball was my sport of choice, when a coach from a different sport approached me about joining that high school team also, I did. He presented a convincing argument about the benefits of cross-training.

Ultimately, I decided to join the team. The coach was right about the strength and conditioning. It did help me on the basketball court. I was also very successful in the other sport, winning the state championship three times.

The local newspaper sportswriters began to notice there may be some truth to what my coach was telling me.

"You're a blue-chip athlete, Gamble. Do you know what that means?" Coach Reynolds asked.

"No, I'm not sure what that means," I said, wanting to learn more.

"It means you're going to be a Division I athlete in college. You're going to be able to pick what school you want to go to," he said with enthusiasm and excitement.

I had big dreams, and some of the coaches I played for knew what I wanted to achieve. I wanted more than anything to become an Olympic athlete. It wasn't like I didn't think I could accomplish my goals, but hearing them from a coach made me feel validated that I was a good athlete, and I didn't always get that kind of acknowledgment from other people. I had only made the honorable mention All-State team in basketball my sophomore year of high school. Two years later, I was a consensus All-American, one of the top five players in the country, recruited nationally and player of the year in West Virginia. Maybe the sportswriters who voted for All-State my sophomore year overlooked me?

Nonetheless, I never once publicly acknowledged Coach Reynolds for helping me reach my dreams. Why? Because while I suppressed the memories from the three other sexual assaults, I never forgot the day in the summer of my sophomore year Coach Reynolds sexually assaulted me. Although it took time to put words to what happened, I suspected for many years what happened to me was wrong on so many levels.

During the summer of 1981, Coach Reynolds and I were in the weight room working out together. No one else was around. After finishing our last set of reps, he called me over to him as he picked up his large, jingling keyring. There were so many keys on that ring, they bulged outward in his pocket.

"Come here for a minute," he said as he hurriedly found the key to open the door between the weight room and the auditorium. He reached back for my hand, a similar gesture I'd experienced twice before, once by Joe and the other by the groomsman. Neither of those times had a good outcome.

We walked into the auditorium, and he led me toward the middle of the rows and told me to sit down on the floor. I was frozen in the moment. I wasn't terrified or afraid, I was just stunned, wondering what was happening. The auditorium wasn't pitch black. I'm just not sure where the sliver of light was coming from. I could see his eyes. Brown eyes. The same eyes I'd drawn numerous times on a watercolor drawing twenty-four years later when I started sexual abuse therapy with Belinda in Arizona, without making the connection to the source of the trauma until the summer of 2008.

My cheek touched up against his scratchy, unshaven face. The same face I'd repeatedly drawn subconsciously nine years later on a notepad during my work annual meetings without making the connection at the time to the sexual assault I'd experienced. When a person experiences a traumatic event, the "thinking brain" goes offline. Very often, this is why I didn't have the words to describe what happened to me.

On that summer day in 1981, the ultimate betrayal between an athlete and her coach took place and added to my list of traumatic events I would have to process years later.

It was betrayal on a new scale. I trusted him implicitly with my dreams and my desire to play sports at the next level. He convinced me if I did weight training with him it would help me tremendously in basketball. He was right about that. It did give me a competitive advantage over some athletes at that time because it wasn't as acceptable for women to lift weights. He was a pioneer in many ways. He was also a very good coach— encouraging, positive, and would acknowledge when I did something he felt was extraordinary.

I remember one day he brought me a pile of *Glamour* magazines and told me to see how the women in the magazines dressed. He suggested I should emulate them. These types of conversations made me uncomfortable and increased my self-consciousness about my developing body. Later in life, this led to body image issues that would take me years to overcome.

I wish I could say the sexual abuse by Coach Reynolds happened *only* one time, which of course would be one time too many. However, there were six other incidents, most of which occurred while I was with my two good friends and drinking buddies, Leah and Pam. We were all in high school, and they were both one year older than me. We would find a legal adult to buy us beer and liquor and got into a bad habit of driving around and binge drinking. Pam was the whisky drinker. Leah and I drank the beer. Somehow, Leah always knew where Coach Reynolds was going to be hanging out. She would say, "Let's go drink some beers with Reynolds." Pam and I would be well on our way to getting a buzz and pretty much agree to anything.

There were a group of coaches from the high school who would hang out on weekend nights and drink. The first time the three of us showed up, the coaches offered us more beer. I remember all of us being showered with attention. Responsible teachers and coaches would have assured that three young high school girls who had been drinking would be safely escorted home. Instead, at least two of us became victims of sexual abuse.

There is no question the alcohol clouded my judgment and eliminated most of my ability to make better decisions. I was also a teenager with a developing brain who quite naturally did impulsive things and didn't always make the best decisions. While I was going through trauma therapy, I had to come to terms with the guilt I felt about putting myself in dangerous situations.

In high school, I would spend most of my mornings before the bell rang for classes to start standing by Coach Reynolds in the hallway, talking to him and a couple other coaches who had hall duty. While in high school, I wasn't making the connection with the sexual assaults I'd experienced. It was like I didn't even realize at the time how wrong what he had done to me was. I seemed to enjoy being around him until he started sexually harassing me in school. It was like a lightbulb went off in my head, and I began to realize what was happening to me was not okay.

One day in the school lunchroom, Coach Reynolds sat on an upside-down plastic milk crate and sold milk to students. He called me over and said, "Gamble, you ever heard of the withdrawal method? It will keep you from getting pregnant." He continued harassing me and calling after me as I walked quickly out of the lunchroom and went to the library. I felt so uncomfortable with his comments.

Somewhere between the beginning and end of my senior year in high school, I realized what he had done was so wrong on so many different levels. He disgusted me. I stayed away from him as much as possible. I still participated on the team, but I didn't want anything to do with him, and he pretty much stayed away from me, not coaching me like he had in the first two years.

~

I kept a watercolor drawing I did in the summer of 2008 and showed it to my mother after a conversation we had one day. She said, "That really resembles your coach." It proved to me my subconscious mind had a way of showing me what I needed to see. Putting the image on paper moved the memory to a place where I could acknowledge the trauma.

In hindsight, I recognize participating in underage drinking had dire consequences for me on more than one occasion. I immensely regret those actions and behaviors. Even if people blamed me for what happened to me outside of the school grounds, I could still point to the initial incident where I did nothing to "ask for" being sexually abused. I would have hoped that a responsible, trusted coach would not have made decisions that would have hurt me. The tendency is for a victim to be blamed. After years of trauma therapy, I can say with full confidence it was not my fault.

~

Given the frequency and intensity of all the flashbacks I had between 2005 and 2008, it's not a big leap to say I experienced some type of trauma in one way or another during my stays at Joe's house. It's one of those situations where I have learned to accept I had traumatic experiences without total recall. In some ways, I was spared additional pain, and in other ways the often painful, fearful flashbacks brought to life pure terror, interfering with my present and often leaving me with clues, but no definitive explanations.

Over the years, I would see Joe periodically when he came to town for a visit or at some family gathering. Our conversations would begin like this just about every time I saw him.

"Hi, Aim. How ya doin'? Joe would ask.

"Doing fine. How are you?" I would answer with an intentionally upbeat tone of voice.

"Doing pretty good." And Joe would laugh. Maybe it was a nervous laugh.

I'd find myself sitting in a corner of the room, mind wandering to why Joe would ever do something like that to me. The conversation around me would continue, and I would just disconnect into a world of my own private thoughts, while everyone around me treated Joe as if he had never done anything wrong, even though almost everyone knew what he had done. This was for sure an example of having my feelings discounted. I had to learn how to honor my own truth.

It was one thing being an adult who had gone through significant trauma therapy to sit in a room with my abuser. It was another thing when I was a child and was expected to interact with Joe as if nothing ever happened. This is probably one of the reasons I had suppressed the memories so significantly.

At a young age, however, what helped me cope with the adversity I experienced was having older sisters who loved me and cared about me. They made sure I had an abundance of toys growing up, since I was fondly referred to as the "baby" of the family. All the older kids and adults were always buying me some type of toy. I distinctly remember taking a crayon and drawing on my Raggedy Ann doll all the places I'd been sexually violated. I don't remember what age I was when I did that, but I do recall I was quite young. In the summer of 2008, this memory became much more apparent and relevant as I processed traumatic memories. While the sexual abuse by Joe ended when I was nine, the expectation of secrecy and silence prevailed. My mother threw my Raggedy Ann doll in the trash shortly after I revealed the sexual abuse. It stood out in my mind as I revisited the memories in that summer, that the "toys do talk," and in this case even the toys had to be silenced.

The whole idea that I was expected not to bring up the topic or my experience with sexual abuse is one of the reasons it made such an impact on me when I purchased the video camera and adamantly stated I was going to "speak my truth." Making the videos was my way of expressing the dark truths that were silenced for so many years and only spoken out loud to my childhood stuffed animal, Rabbie.

In the summer of 2008, I began my journey of ending my silence and, in a sense, demanding to be heard. The video camera capturing my voice was my first step in articulating the traumas, how they affected me, and what I did to cope.

As I watched the videos fifteen years later, they left me with a roadmap back in time to glance at every now and then and see just how far I had come. Watching myself speak in many different character voices and my own voice made me feel pleased and grateful I had gone to Best Buy on that June day in 2008 and purchased that camera.

Chapter 8

When I started filming the videos with Rabbie in 2008, it wasn't unusual for me to think I could lean on my imagination for stress relief and tell a story about what I was experiencing. I really wanted to write a script for my movie, but I realized I couldn't concentrate enough to write. The flashbacks were taking a toll on my ability to use the screenwriting software I had purchased. I didn't have any experience writing a screenplay, but I believed I could do it with the help of a guided program. I had heard about other people who had been successful, even though they had little or no experience, so I thought, "Why not give it a try."

Initially, my vision was to tell my story from Chance's perspective. I envisioned having the stuffed black dog be the narrator to tell my story. Chance, my black lab, had been with me for over fifteen years. I imagined if Chance could talk, she'd definitely have some incredible insights to share. What would Chance have to say about the high drama day in Arizona, as she ran to me in the front yard and licked my face?

When I turned on the camera, Rabbie just seemed to have so much to say. Rabbie's character was my inner mentor, my internal voice of wisdom and the humorous side of me.

I don't recall who bought Shasta the white, stuffed rabbit toy. Shelley was known to show up at my house with new toys and treats for the dogs. The dogs tended to have lots of toys. It could, however, have been my subconscious mind who recognized the significance of a white stuffed rabbit who provided a significant amount of comfort to the little girl inside me. Or it could have been Shelley's subconscious mind reminding her of giving a gift to her little sister. I never thought anything about the white rabbit until the day I started filming my movie and inherently called the rabbit "Rabbie."

The deciding factor for Rabbie to be the narrator was Shasta, because she wouldn't give me the stuffed dog toy. But as it turns out, Rabbie's character was spewing out my sometimes playful and sometimes sarcastic sense of humor. I would come to learn in time how I used my sense of humor to cope and just how important having those three dogs was to me. They even sparked comedy relief. Laughter was a break in the stark and sometimes dark memories lurking in the past, but ever present through my flashbacks. Even in times of darkness, as my sister Shelley always says, "You gotta laugh!"

It's only in retrospect that I can see how all the props, including the tractor, and characters in my movie scenes played a role in my life, sometimes in some symbolic way or another. The creativity gave me the freedom of expression and an outlet to keep myself as sane as possible while I dove deeper and deeper into my past traumas.

The very first therapist I ever saw many years prior had told me I'd need to find my way and understand myself better by slowly peeling back the layers. She told me to imagine how I peeled an onion. One layer at a time and, in my case, I had many layers to cut through. Though some part of me would like to place blame with Kendra for chopping the layers, instead of peeling them back slowly, I think I simply had so much trauma it was beyond standing in the ocean during high tide. It was much more like being in the middle of a tsunami. There is, however, research that shows sometimes when a therapist has a client give details of traumatic events it can overwhelm a person and trigger an onslaught of flashbacks, making a situation much worse and not resolving the issue. At the very least, it seems "chopping" the layers contributed to making my situation worse and not better.

I had been attempting to unravel my layers at a young age. I was the seventh-grade kid who read *The Road Less Traveled* by M. Scott Peck and *Man's Search for Meaning* by Viktor Frankl. To say I was deep is an understatement. I simply had this overwhelming desire to understand.

Looking back, I would say it was very helpful to me to read stories of how other people overcame great suffering. I was inspired by them. Having been sexually abused at such a young age, I had to grow up rather quickly. I never had therapy as a child, but years later, after my mom witnessed the hell I went through, she admitted to me she thought I should have had therapy, and she regretted not taking me to see someone. I just don't think she realized how damaging and traumatic the sexual abuse I experienced was. I also think it speaks to the complexity of the issue itself. But that hindsight thing often shows us when we feel like we *should have* done something different. If given the opportunity to go back in time, we'd change some of the things we did or didn't do. None of us get the benefit of hindsight to change the past, but perhaps get some comfort in the acknowledgment of what may have been the right thing to do.

~

Between being outside and filming my scenes, I spent a great deal of time in the house. While I went to the doctor's, grocery store, bagel shop, Starbucks, and local bookstore, I felt most comfortable at home. Because I had been unable to leave my home much during my probation period, I was still adapting to having my freedom back. I was also trying to learn what may trigger my flashbacks, but sometimes there was simply no warning. They could come out of nowhere. I had to make the best of it, so I set up sort of self-help rooms in my house.

My dining room table was covered with art materials—markers, watercolors, and lots of different sizes of colored paper. As much as I regretted Susan influencing me to start sexual abuse counseling, I did find her recommendation of the watercolors helpful.

In the dining room, I had a large, round, wooden table with a beautiful starburst in the light brown wood. It was another one of my safe spaces where I allowed myself great latitude in capturing wherever my thoughts and creative ability took me.

Some would say I must have been manic because I was experiencing so much creativity. I'm not really sure if I was or wasn't manic. In my video footage, I'm very lucid. I was taking mood stabilizing medications that were keeping the bipolar disorder in check, I think. But I did have a great deal of anxiety, and as noted before, it sometimes triggered hypomania. I'm just not willing to give all the credit for my creative talents to a mental illness. It just seems wrong to me.

When I wasn't using art as a coping mechanism, I was playing the piano or drums. I purchased the drum set in the summer of 2008 at a local music store.

I had discovered the idea of using a drum set in one of the books I was reading about healing from sexual abuse. They suggested using drums as a healthy way to deal with anger. Very often I would turn on the video camera and record my drum and piano playing sessions. When I felt angry, I would sit and bang away, while I talked to the camera about what I was thinking and feeling. One drumming session, I said, "*It's time to play the drums and work out my frustration. I feel those sensations on a daily basis when I have to remember that bullshit. Do you know what the video tape is for? The tape is for me so I can speak my truth without someone telling me that it's been such a long time ago. Do they think I want to remember this shit? Well, by God, that young person never had a chance to speak. But I do now.*"

Those musical instruments were great healthy outlets. The piano keyboard was in the living room my mom had painted for me. I had been playing the piano frequently for years. The drums, on the other hand, I hadn't a clue how to play them. I could sit and attempt to keep a beat with a certain cadence, and I did love to use the cymbal. When I was a kid, I'd take books and set them up like drums. I used two wide pencils with orange erasers as my drumsticks. I would pound on those books until Mom came in my room and told me to stop. I'd beg her to get me a set of drums, but she said I'd drive her "crazy" with all that noise.

I found the drums and piano a great way to cope. I played the piano when I felt peaceful, often improvising various tunes and using the video camera to record myself. The video camera was almost like a witness and an audience all in one that captured part of my healing journey.

The room where I spent a lot of my time was right off the kitchen. It had a brown leather couch, a blue suede lounger, a non-working fireplace, television, drum set, and a rarely used exercise bike. I hardly ever turned on the television, but I did enjoy the music stations. I would latch on to some of the lyrics in songs and use them for inspiration and motivation.

It's not lost on me how many resources, skills, background knowledge, and positive experiences I had to build on. In some ways, it was like reaching into a large toolbox and finding the right tool to use in an instant. Sometimes I needed a hammer, and sometimes I needed a nail. The key was to go with the flow and determine what to use and when to use it. At the end of the day, I needed every single tool I had to recover.

~

In my eighth day of filming in June, I turned the camera on myself. It was shortly after a therapy session, and I left completely distraught. After telling her about the sexual abuse I experienced in a previous therapy session, I mentioned to Kendra my mom had given me the letter I wrote to her, and I'd kept it in a notebook for years. Kendra asked if I minded sharing the letter with her, and when I did, she made a copy of it for her files.

After reading the letter, Kendra asked me a series of questions regarding physical abuse. I was a bit confused because the letter I'd given her related only to the sexual abuse I had experienced from Joe. There was no other mention of anyone else in my family, and I'd never brought up being physically abused by anyone. Kendra made an assumption that I had experienced other abuse, probably based on what she had seen with other clients. Even though I told her I wasn't physically abused by anyone, she began a series of questions.

Kendra asked, "Do you have any scars on your body?"

"Only the ones from playing sports and the spider bite I got in Germany," I replied as I slouched into the chair, feeling defensive.

"Do you have any scars on your head?" she said, as if interrogating me.

"Only a birthmark," I answered. I wasn't sure where she was taking the conversation. I felt anxious, uncomfortable, and was fearing the worst with her line of questioning. I put my head down, slouched my shoulders forward, and leaned my elbows on my knees.

"Let me see it," she demanded.

I lifted my hair so she could see the birthmark, and she immediately reacted. "That's no birthmark. Is that what they told you? Someone pulled your hair out at birth."

I was shocked and stunned by Kendra's comment. I pushed back. "No. It's a birthmark," I said emphatically.

"I'm sorry, Amy, your family's been lying to you." Kendra emphasized her point.

I put my face in my hands and shook my head. It seemed the therapy appointment ended without me being left whole. Then again, I'm not so sure how a therapist could leave someone whole after telling her a support system she relied on pulled her hair out at birth. In that moment, I never questioned how she could know something without any evidence, like a photo from my childhood. She just kind of pulled it out of thin air.

It was late morning, and I left the therapy appointment quivering from the inside out. On my way home, I passed by an outdoor bar and thought "why not stop." I sat on the bar stool and ordered my first of two large margaritas with extra shots of tequila. I hadn't drunk much alcohol in over a year. It was relatively unusual for me at that time in my life to overindulge and get drunk.

As I sat at the outdoor bar, the sun was shining in between the puffy white clouds. I leaned my elbows on top of the bar and stared forward at all the various bottles of liquor neatly placed on the shelves. I could feel my head get a little fuzzy as the alcohol began to take effect. I was an emotional wreck to think someone in my family had done what Kendra said they did to me. But I was also confused because I was always told it was a birthmark on my head. I sat on the bar stool with my thoughts jumping from one side of the argument to the other. "Why would my family do something like that?" "There's no way my family did something like that." "Why would Kendra make that up?" "This is so messed up!"

On that June day, when I got home half drunk, I walked upstairs to the bathroom, took out an electric razor and proceeded to shave the hair off my head. I wanted to see if I had any scars on my head, and I filmed myself doing it. When I separated the hair to expose the birthmark on my head, pointing at it, I said,

"*That...that's child abuse. Oh, my...holy shit!*" I was really in shock looking at the birthmark in a way I'd never looked at it before. Never once did it enter my mind that I had been abused as a child. And now my mind was polluted with dark thoughts about my family that I never had until Kendra made her comment.

Even though I didn't want to believe Kendra, after having been in therapy with her for over a year, we had developed a trusting therapeutic relationship. I didn't think at the time she would be creating a false story. I didn't even know there was such a thing as a false story.

When I shaved my head, it didn't feel like a self-destructive moment at the time. I kept repeating into the camera, "Let's see what other scars I have on my head." I was in the mode of discovering if there was any truth to the comment Kendra made to me, and I was curious to see what else I could find under my hair. I had to see for myself. It's kind of obvious being drunk didn't help my judgment, and in my state of mind I didn't consider how that would affect my ability to return to work. I had planned on returning by August 2008. When I shaved my head, I never thought how it may look to other people. I just took my hair off one section at a time, shaving it all the way down to my scalp and leaving a couple of random strands of hair for some unknown reason.

I was alone with my three dogs and there was no one for me to talk to, so I got back in my car and drove to Kendra's office. I marched in, lip quivering, gasping for breath in between crying and holding my breath. I demanded the receptionist let me see Kendra. The receptionist dropped her mouth open and looked at me with wide eyes, as I looked quite a bit different in that moment compared to how I looked during my mid-morning appointment.

Kendra came out and waved me back to her office.

She took one look at me and said, "Amy, why did you do this to yourself?"

As I continued crying, I said, "Because I wanted to see if there were any scars on my head that I might not know about."

Kendra paused and then said, "Amy, would you be willing to go to the hospital? I'm going to call an ambulance."

"Yes," I said, sobbing, "I'll go to the hospital."

"Have you been drinking?" Kendra asked, even though I'm

sure she could smell the alcohol.

"Yes, I've been drinking," I said, choking back the tears.

"Amy, you just can't drink while going through this kind of therapy. It's not good for you. And now look what you did to your hair," she said in a shaming tone of voice as she walked out the door and asked the receptionist to call for an ambulance.

About twenty minutes passed, then two police officers came into the office along with the EMTs. Kendra said, "I called for an ambulance, not the police."

One officer said, "Is she willing to go voluntarily?"

Kendra answered, "Yes, she'll go in the ambulance."

The EMTs took me on each side of my arms and led me to the ambulance. They took me to a local psychiatric hospital. When we arrived, they put me into a small holding room so they could evaluate me, which meant watch me to make sure my behaviors weren't life threatening. I lay down on the dirty carpet, because the only thing in the room was a chair. I smelled the must in the room, and it made me sick to my stomach as it triggered memories about what Joe had done to me. I felt numb. Numb from the alcohol, numb from all the traumatic memories. I was over it all. I didn't want to talk to the intake nurse or tell them why I shaved my head. The last thing I needed was a lecture from the nurse on how self-destructive my behaviors were. After a short while, I went to sleep.

Once I was moved to the psych unit, I called my mom and asked her to go take care of my dogs. They put me in room right next to the nurse's station, so they could make certain I wouldn't harm myself. Because of my self-destructive behavior, they thought I may be suicidal, which I wasn't. It wasn't a private room, but I didn't have a roommate for the two days I was there.

I hadn't yet told my mom what Kendra had said my family did. She came up to my home and stayed at my house until I was released from the hospital a couple of days later. My mom stayed with me for a few days and helped me with household chores and taking care of my dogs.

"Why did you shave your head?" she asked, not looking at me with judgment, but with sad eyes. It must have been difficult for her to see me in such emotional pain.

"Kendra told me you guys pulled my hair out at birth," I said, very disconnected and unemotional.

"No one did that to you. It's a birthmark. Your therapist is crazy, and she's putting lies into your head," she said, almost pleading with me to believe her. "That kind of statement can ruin a person's life."

I did believe my mother, and I didn't believe her. It would take me a very long time to resolve the conflict in my head.

I went back to see Kendra shortly after I was released from the psych unit. She was surprised to see me, even though I had several appointments on the books in advance.

"They let you out already? I thought they'd keep you longer." She raised her brow as if confused.

"Yep. They let me out. They really didn't do anything for me," I said without much emotion, and feeling despondent, as if I was beaten down.

"Oh, Amy," Kendra said disapprovingly.

I wasn't really sure how much I could trust Kendra, but I was reliant upon her for emotional support. I felt like I didn't have much choice in whether or not I continued to see her. There was a part of me which recognized how much she had helped me, mostly with teaching me about trauma and coping strategies. I found myself in a familiar situation that I had been in most of my life. Even if someone did something questionable, hurtful, or even horrible, I believed at the time I had no choice but to focus on the good the person brought into my life. At the very least, it was how I coped, and at the very most, it was my survival mechanism.

I continued to see Kendra, even though I had some serious questions about what she said about my family.

Following my release from the hospital, I went upstairs and, in front of the mirror, videotaped myself talking into the camera. While my reflection is captured on the video, these are the words I said:

"I know who I am. I know I'm Amy Gamble. I know I'm forty-three years old." In between sobs, I continue, *"Part of getting well is knowing what you're dealing with. The only way to get the right help is to be vulnerable in a system you don't trust. But I'll be damned, if it takes me a lifetime, I will get well. I know I've been severely traumatized. Only by the hand of God have I survived. Only by the hand of God. It's truly a miracle."*

It took me years to watch that part of the video. I could tell I was attempting to ground myself in the present moment by stating my name and age, because at the time my brain had been flooded with so many traumatic memories. It was difficult to imagine the people I relied on for love and support could hurt me like Kendra said they did. For a long time, I couldn't bear to see myself in so much emotional pain. The emotion that struck me the most after I watched that part of the video was disappointment. A sort of deep sadness for that period in my life. Even when I tried to help myself by reaching out to professionals, I still managed to find someone who helped me, but hurt me too.

I never really wanted to believe Kendra, but her planting that seed always created a question in my mind. "Was my family telling me the truth?" About ten years after the time I shaved my head, I went to a medical doctor and found out I had a nevus sebaceous birthmark on my head. It became irritated, and I ended up needing surgery to remove it. It turns out this type of birthmark is fairly common. I was relieved and yet angry with Kendra when I found out definitively it was a birthmark. I was pleased my instinct was correct in knowing I never experienced child abuse, like Kendra had suggested. However, it brought up emotions I had to process. It was another person I would fight myself internally to forgive. Another reason not to trust people for fear they might hurt me. Another trust issue to work through. Another matter to accept. Though I had forgotten about the comment Kendra made to me, I was reminded of how much turmoil her comment caused. When I saw the medical doctor, it brought up memories from the past. I remember thinking, "When is this shit ever going to end?" The shitstorm a professional therapist created.

Chapter 9

In the beginning of July 2008, my sister Shelley came to spend the night with me. She kept calling and checking on me, even though I was insistent that I didn't want anyone from my family in my personal space. Shelley knew from talking to my mother what Kendra had said to me about my family pulling my hair out at birth. Shelley said, "This is completely untrue. It's a birthmark. Always has been, always will be." I wanted to believe Shelley, but I still had my doubts.

When I woke up the morning of Shelley's visit, I was drawn to the kitchen by the smell of bacon cooking. I came down the stairs and glanced at the floor and saw Buddy, Shasta, and Chance each had their own paper plate filled with eggs and bacon and were eagerly enjoying their special meal.

I stood in the kitchen watching Shelley cook the breakfast and proceeded to pick up the video camera, start filming, and picked up Rabbie from the basket of dog toys. In a moment of silliness, in my Rabbie voice, I had a conversation with my sister.

"Oh, my, someone is cooking, and it brought me right out of my little basket," I said to my sister in Rabbie's voice.

Shelley raised her eyebrows and pushed her glasses up on her nose. She smiled awkwardly and played along.

"Who is that? Oh, my goodness, that's who brought Rabbie home from the store. Yippee! She came to visit. Do you think she'll meet me even though I'm not like the *real* Rabbie?" I asked in my Rabbie voice.

In my own voice, I said, "I don't know. You can ask her."

I bounced Rabbie on Shelley's back and said, "Hi! Hi! Hi, Shelley."

Shelley took a step back away from the stove, glanced at me quickly, and then looked at Rabbie. She smiled and said, "Hi, Rabbie. What's happening?"

"I'm Rabbie! I'm Rabbie. I want to give you kisses! You saved Jamie Northwood's life."

I noticed many years later while watching the video I referred to myself as Jamie and not Amy. There was a time when I had considered changing my name. I had read that sometimes when people realize the effects of abuse, they may decide to change their name to create a new identity and put some emotional distance between the past and the present. My motivation was driven off the anger stimulated by what Kendra had said to me. The cascading emotional slide I experienced from her comments was like taking a knife to a scar and making it a wound. Even though I struggled internally with whether or not to believe Kendra—it did unfortunately take me years to heal from the seed she planted in my mind. It was hard to forget something so horrific. It had such a lasting negative impact on my mind and in my spirit and drove me to want to change my name and disappear.

Because Shelley had given me the stuffed rabbit I talked to in childhood, I felt like it had made a significant impact on my life. Talking to the toy gave me an emotional outlet as a nine-year-old kid confiding the sexual abuse I had experienced. In the summer of 2008, I came to realize how consequential it was for me to have had someone to talk to, allowing me to put words to the memories, even if that someone was a stuffed toy. As I traveled down my healing journey and came to recognize the seriousness of the abuse, I felt like my path in life could have turned out much differently. My dramatic self felt like Shelley had saved my life in some way.

As I called myself a different name while videotaping, Shelley played along. I tossed Rabbie back into the basket, and we continued to carry on a conversation I recorded about my niece Natalie's birthday, dog sitting, and interacted about my dogs' reactions to the breakfast they had. Watching the video reminds me of how we found a slice of fun and silliness in the midst of trudging through my emotional chaos.

It also struck me that Shelley wasn't judging my process of coping. I know she wasn't aware of all the traumatic experiences I had been through, but she did know about several. Shelley was the sister who ran after the truck trying to save me from the groomsman. I wasn't keeping any secrets about why I was in counseling. But she never commented on my hair or dwelled on the fact I shaved my head. She was just showing up and offering her support in the ways she felt comfortable. Shelley had been supporting me for as long as I can remember. She was the sister who showed up in good times and bad times. Our relationship had always been one of mutual support and understanding.

~

A few days after Shelley went back home, I captured on film the guys who came to my house to renovate my kitchen. I'm not sure what inspired me to rebuild my kitchen, but that's what I did. The entire kitchen was given a complete overhaul—new cabinets, new range, new countertop, and new flooring. I spared no expense to bring the kitchen up to date, even though my short-term disability had not been approved, which meant I had no income. Not really a wise decision. But it was really beautiful when finished. It provided me with a joyful space and a significant upgrade to the aging kitchen. It also symbolically represented a part of me that was healing, though the journey would be more like a one-hundred-ten-mile ultra-marathon, and I was on mile one.

In the three days it took the guys to work on the kitchen, my mother came up to visit. I captured our short conversation on video.

My mother walked into the kitchen and asked, "Are you ready to go?"

"Yep," I answered as I filmed the knocked down wall between the kitchen and den and all the unfinished wiring hanging from the walls.

"What do you have to snack on?" my mother asked as she walked farther into the kitchen.

"I don't know. Look in the pantry," I answered as she walked over to the pantry doors to look inside.

"Let's go shopping," she said as I ended the video clip.

We went out together to do some shopping. This says to me I was battling back the false statement the therapist put in my head. Although at the time I was conflicted by what the truth was, I was trying to remember my mom almost always attempted to have my best interest at heart. I had always had a good relationship with my mother. She was the person I went to for support and encouragement. She was the loudest voice of positive encouragement, and she believed me when I said I was going to accomplish something. We made many memories together. Because of our strong bond, the comment by Kendra hurt even more significantly.

A few days later in July 2008, I was outside again filming on my "movie set." This time, the set had become sort of a mound in my backyard. Both my sister and mother had seen the mound when they came to visit me, but no one really asked me what I was doing. I had been piling up dirt for a few weeks. When I began digging, I didn't set out to build a mound. I began cleaning up the backyard and leveling the uneven ground with my orange tractor. Then, who knows what went through my mind. Digging was very therapeutic. Sort of a mindless activity, and God knows I needed some of that.

By the time Shelley and my mom saw my makeshift mound, it was fairly sizeable. I had taken the tractor and dug a huge hole, piling up the dirt and stacking it until it took the shape of a mound. When it was all said and done, the pile was about eight feet high from the ground up.

The mound was in the background of the video I had made for Kendra. When I showed Kendra the video with my tractor in the backyard, she glanced up from the camera and looked at me with disapproval, so I turned the camera off and never mentioned anything to her about what I was doing in my backyard again. I just assumed she saw my big pile and didn't approve of it.

In one scene I was filming, I have Rabbie sitting on the mound with a pair of sunglasses on and one eye exposed. In my Rabbie voice, I asked, "What the hell are you doing, Amy?"

I laughed into the camera and said, "I don't really know. I'll let you know when it's done."

"What do you mean, when it's done? What in the world is this thing?" my Rabbie voice asked, and I realized at the time piling up a huge amount of dirt in my backyard looked rather strange.

I just started laughing on camera. Laughing at myself building a freaking mound in my backyard. I knew at the time it was more than unusual to do such a thing. But I was trying to cope and keep myself safe. Because that's what Kendra told me to do—"Keep yourself safe, Amy."

I was occupying my mind with extreme creativity. I needed an escape from the traumatic flashbacks and intrusive memories. After my head shaving incident, the strongest thing I was drinking was a cup of Starbuck's bold coffee with a little cream. It appeared from watching the videos I may have learned my lesson about getting drunk. It seemed nothing good came with overindulging on any kind of alcohol, and I had plenty of data points in my history to come to that conclusion. I did, however, need an escape. I needed a way to relieve my brain from the perpetual dripping faucet of deep sadness. I had to try to shift my mind from constantly processing disturbing memories and give myself some feeling of joy. Ultimately, I decided to turn to my inner child's imagination. It wasn't so much a deliberate thought as it was a dancing idea which floated into my brain, and I latched on to it.

A lot of my creativity came from watching the theatre, which allowed me to connect to my emotions. I found this out when I saw my first Broadway show, *Evita*, in New York City my senior year of high school. My sister Cindy and I went to visit my friend Mel. He was a huge women's basketball fan and sportswriter. I met him during a basketball try-out for a National Sports Festival Team in my junior year of high school. The National Sports Festival was a mini-Olympics held every year except an Olympic year. The country was divided into four regions—East, South, North, and West. I was one of the youngest players in the country to make the East team. From that point on, Mel and I became good friends. He may have been a bit biased when he selected me as the high school girls' basketball "Player of the Year" for the entire country for a sports magazine he wrote for. I was pretty good, but probably not that good.

On that cold December day, Mel, Cindy, and I went down to the theatre on New Year's Eve, turning the calendar to 1983. We took the subway from Queens to Manhattan, and that alone was a memorable experience, considering I was a small-town girl who grew up on a farm. We were far from Times Square where the ball dropped, to not be in a massive crowd of people. From that night forward, I was hooked on theatre.

I've seen a number of shows on and off Broadway over the years, but first saw *Wicked* in 2005 in New York City about a month before I had started sexual abuse therapy. I was mesmerized as I sat watching. I purchased piano music with lyrics from the show. I had been playing the music and imagining what it was all about. The words were ever so powerful, and put to music, it moved my soul.

In my backyard, what was I doing besides keeping myself safe? I was digging and piling up the dirt. Really, the "digging" part is a parallel to what I was doing in therapy—digging up past traumas that were not on the surface, but deep inside my subconscious. I'm not so sure digging was such a good idea in either case. But piling up dirt, old bricks the previous owner had left behind, and pieces of decaying trees—this was unsightly in my backyard, but it was an interesting endeavor.

As the days passed, I added various parts to the mound. One section had a round stainless-steel piece of material used for a fire pit. That was the pit where one of the witch scenes was filmed.

My witch's voice first came to life way back in fourth grade when I tried out for one of the witches in a modified version of Shakespeare's *Macbeth* for the school play. I practiced my witch's voice so much I gave myself a sore throat. But when the time came for me to go before the teachers for the try-out, I became embarrassed and the only thing I did was read the part in a monotone voice—"Double, double, toil and trouble…" Instead of being the witch in the school play, I was a gigantic leaf in a very small Brownie uniform that wasn't mine. One of those highly embarrassing moments in childhood that I now find amusing.

As the years passed, I would frequently employ my witch's voice when joking and playing with my nieces. Everyone thought my witch voice was pretty good. I can say I was deeply inspired by the movie, *The Wizard of Oz*. When I watched the movie when I was younger, the witch scared me, but as I became older, I loved to mimic her voice. I especially liked saying the line, "I'll get you yet, my little pretty, and your little dog too." It always made everyone laugh and still does.

Another example of my witch character came from the very famous Broadway show *Wicked*. The two main characters are both witches. Glenda is the blonde haired, blue eyed, *good witch,* and Elphaba is the green, dark eyed, *bad witch.* As the show progresses, the story shows us how each witch became either good or bad. I tended to focus on the message of how people's perception played a key role in whether something was good or bad.

My life lesson from *Wicked* was learning how much I know, and what I know is neither good or bad, black or white, but rather an eclectic shade of gray. Very often the judgment I pass depends on what filter I'm using when reflecting on a person or experience.

In the beginning of my videos, anything and everything that was bad or what I perceived as evil from my memories and flashbacks became part of the scene with the witch. It was one of the ways I was processing my various emotions. But the witch was no stuffed animal. The witch was me fully dressed in a witch's costume.

Progressing further into my video making, I decided I needed real characters to show a true expression of what I was feeling. I drove a few miles down the road to an older shopping plaza with one of those year-round costume stores. I'd driven by the store several times on my way to the grocery store, but never once thought about going in. I wasn't even a person who went to Halloween parties in costume, let alone buy one to dress up in. But I had an idea, and I was going to follow through with it.

I got out of my car with eager anticipation and a light step as I headed to the store entrance. My eyes kind of lit up like a kid when I saw all the fun costumes. I slowly browsed the aisles with excitement, picking up and touching many different items. I spotted an orange inmate jumpsuit and put that into the cart, along with a pair of plastic handcuffs. I came across a blue police costume with the word "police" stamped in white on top of the upper left pocket. I chose both of those costumes because they reminded me of the Arizona situation, and I was passionate about working out a few things about that experience.

The aisle with a wide variety of witch costumes completely entertained me. I decided on a wig, hat, cape, and broom. The witch had already shown up in voice on the videos, so her costume was a no-brainer. Why I bought the clown outfit with a multi-color wig remains a mystery to me. I guess clowns show a range of emotions and I certainly had a significant range I was dealing with. However, there have been a few movies that have been released since 2008, depicting unhinged people with mental illness dressed as clowns. I seriously doubt I would have ever bought that costume if those movies had been available back then.

The finishing touch to all my costume buying was the face paint. I was going to have so much fun with the face paint. More fun than I could have imagined.

The first time I dressed in full costume for my videotaping session, I put on a base of green face paint and then took red face paint and put it in a ring around my eyes. The red face paint was an expression of pain I felt as I processed various emotions. One time, the witch wore an orange inmate jumpsuit costume with plastic handcuffs hanging from one wrist underneath her black cape, but she always wore her black cape.

At first, Rabbie didn't like it when the witch showed up to be in the videos. But after I taped a couple of scenes with the witch, that all changed. In my Rabbie voice, I commented, "There's not gonna be any evil or bad people in this film. If you're not a good person, you're out! So, witch, you've got to be a *good* witch to stay in this film."

During the summer of 2008, what I came to understand was as a trauma survivor I had to come to terms with seeing my abusers in totality, because in some instances there were good parts to them. In most of my interactions with Mr. Brock, he was really quite friendly and likeable. Until he grabbed me in the store that day, I always found him to be a nice, older man who spoke highly of my grandfather. Joe was always helping everyone out by fixing their cars or changing the oil. For the most part, he was friendly, kind, and considerate.

It might have been one of the most difficult things to come to terms with—how could someone who did something so horrible leave a lasting effect in a positive way too? It kind of put me on an emotional rollercoaster by trying to hold opposite viewpoints in my mind at the same time. What I learned was I'd have to make peace with my polar opposite views by learning to be okay with knowing I would always have conflicting feelings. In order to reconcile my thoughts, I did everything I could to see the evil and the good.

Over ten years after I first put on my green face paint and dressed as a witch, I would come to learn there are specific programs around the country that focus on treating trauma through theatre. In his book, *The Body Keeps the Score*, Dr. Bessel Van Der Kolk says, "Love and hate, aggression and surrender, loyalty and betrayal are the stuff of theatre and the stuff of trauma." Though I wish I could have been in one of the official trauma theatre programs, I found a bit of relief in knowing I wasn't so kooky after all. Taken out of context, what I did to survive trauma therapy, and sometimes bad trauma therapy, may seem a bit out of the ordinary. However, when looked at through the lens of how theatre can allow us to see and feel even the most uncomfortable of emotions, the witch character gave me the opportunity to express myself and process my thinking and emotions in ways which may have been impossible without the help of my imagination. The creation of my witch character let me tap into my strengths and helped me to heal. The witch would say the ugly parts of my truth. She expressed the anger I felt inside as I came to realize how trauma had affected me.

The third and final time I dressed in full makeup as a witch, I took off my black wig and turned directly into the camera and said in my own voice, *"People can say what they want about forgiving, forgetting, and leaving the past behind and all that sort of thing. But the one thing I can tell you is everybody has to heal in their own way and their own time. And telling you to just forget about the past and saying things like that is not supportive. You want to honor your own truth. You want to honor your own timeline. Because only you really know how you feel. Only you really know what those memories are. Only you will feel the pain, only you will feel the joy, and only you will be responsible for your own healing. You can have help and take all the help you can get—take all the support you can get from people—if it's given from the heart. Embrace it. But don't ever let anybody tell you to get over it, let it be, leave it alone—because if it stays inside of you, it will fester into something you don't deserve."*

Although I still had a long way to go in my recovery journey, when I took off the black wig, I turned the page on all the props, toys, and characters I created. All those characters helped me to integrate painful memories. I found when I assigned language to the memories or interrupted the flashbacks, it took the terror away and stopped triggering my fight or flight response.

Looking back, if I hadn't been alone and very isolated for nearly two years, I doubt I would have turned to such an extreme level of creativity. I want to convey how important it was for me to have had such an expansive way to cope. It was for sure an "out of box" way to deal with a flood of traumatic memories.

There was a time when I thought perhaps I was hypomanic, but when I went back and watched the videos, there's no part of me that was in an altered state of mind. Everything I did was done with a deliberate and well thought out method. Not only did I keep myself "safe" during this time, most importantly, I kept myself "sane."

Chapter 10

By the beginning of August 2008, my video making turned into a broader recording of what was happening in my life. On this particular day, I gently knocked from the inside of my front door while filming and said, "I want to give mama robin a warning before I open the door." A robin made her nest and laid three blue eggs on the wreath Shelley had made for my front door. The baby birds had hatched successfully and had grown their brown speckled feathers. They lay crowded together in a fairly large nest.

I slowly opened the door, and the robin flew out of the nest and landed on a small pine tree in my front yard. She was always somewhere close watching her babies. I imagined nature was coming to me as if to say, "Don't worry, Amy. Everything is going to be okay. We're here cheering you on." It gave me great peace and joy to see nature's beauty up close and personal. I found a slice of healing and comfort in seeing those baby birds.

Outside of my family, I didn't have many friends. I met Leon at the local bank, and he and I became friends. He came to my house for a visit in the second week of August. We talked about why I was filming my experience.

"What's your point of making these videos?" Leon asked as we sat around the big round table where I cleared off all of the art materials.

"My point is to reach other people who may have been impacted by sexual abuse, so they'll know they aren't alone," I answered with a confident and clear tone of voice.

"Well, that seems reasonable," he said with his banker-like, matter of fact left brain. "I think you should talk on camera and say how you feel. Talk about your flashbacks and show yourself on camera." While I had been doing what Leon suggested, his words reinforced my desire to keep filming my experience and provided validation for documenting my journey.

It was also a bit of a relief to see another human being, since by the time August came around, I had told my mother not to visit me for a while, and for the most part she had abided by my wishes. I was still very much bothered by Kendra's comments. The only consolation was I still had my three dogs to keep me company, and my pesky neighbor who lived to the left of me about a half a football field away.

I remember the day my neighbor came in my backyard uninvited.

"What are you doing, Amy?" Mr. Williams asked.

"Well, today I'm doing some filming again," I answered with a slight hesitation, wondering if he was going to get to his point of asking me for what he wanted, since that was generally his motivation for showing up. Meanwhile, his nosy wife would peek behind her curtains and gawk at me anytime I was in the yard. I suppose from the outside looking in, I might have provided some level of entertainment, given I spent the majority of my time in the summer of 2008 outside in the backyard with a camera.

"I was wondering, Amy," he began his request, "can we have that wood down at the end of your yard for firewood? I can send my grandkids over to pick it up."

"Yes, you can have it." I was relieved he got to what he wanted and anxious for him to move on.

My dogs were friendly, and even they didn't like him. They'd kind of lined up behind me and lain down when he came in the yard, as if they were literally watching my back. I just had one of those intuitive feelings about him which evoked a kind of creepy impression. Then again, a lot of people gave me the creeps while I was going through trauma therapy. It was a little hard to trust my judgment about other people, though my instincts seemed to usually be correct. They were survival instincts I had learned at a very young age.

The next time my neighbor came into my yard was when I

brought my RV back from West Virginia. I had stored it on my sister's farm in the hayfield I used to play in with the tractor. I had literally just parked the RV in the side yard in between large pine trees and below the driveway. I opened the door to let the dogs out and there he was, lurking outside the door.

"Can I see your RV?" he said.

"Well, since you're here, I guess so." I reluctantly let him in the door. He went into the main room of the RV equipped with a couch, chair, and kitchen area. He walked into the back and saw the queen size bed and cabinets. I walked out and put my hand on the outside door just in case I needed to exit quickly. The trauma therapy had made me overly sensitive to what may be perceived as potential danger.

"Are you taking a trip soon?" he asked as he stepped out of the RV.

"I'm thinking about it," I said cautiously, not wanting to give him too much information. He was one of the few people I interacted with during this time, and his demeanor made me nervous.

He slowly got out and started to walk back toward his house, then turned around and took one more look at me. I turned and called for the dogs to come with me.

I took the KOA campground book out of the RV, which was about as big as an old-fashioned yellow pages book, and put it on the dining room table. I started looking through the book to see if any place piqued my interest. I was excited to be planning a trip.

I had been reading stories on the internet of people who had survived sexual abuse or sexual assault and came across a story about an actress and film writer named Angela Shelton, who had taken a cross-country trip in an RV and made a documentary out of her experiences. She had researched and found several women with her same first and last name in different places around the country.

As she met and interviewed the women, she determined over seventy percent of them had also been sexually abused, raped, or been a victim of domestic violence. Ultimately, her trip was very healing and demonstrated she was not alone in her own journey with a mission to reclaim her life and heal from her wounds.

I was inspired by her story and thought, "I'd like to take a healing cross-country trip." It sounded like a good idea to me. I had already taken several cross-country trips in the RV, most with my mother, one with a cousin, and every trip with my three dogs.

One of the really unusual things about sitting at my table and planning a trip was that I didn't ask anyone to go with me or tell anyone where I was going, not even Kendra. I wanted to shut down all the loud noise in my head of conflicting thoughts and views on whether or not my family actually pulled my hair out at birth or if Kendra really knew what the hell she was talking about. But I did film the various stages of preparing for the trip.

I did take my dogs with me. They were travel dogs. I'd say they probably traveled to more states than the average person. All I had to do was say, "Do you want to go?" They'd all jump up, get a big sparkle in their eyes, and start wagging their tails. Chance would always whine and go get a toy in her mouth. This was her way of communicating excitement.

Before I left on my few weeks' trip across the country, I spent time having the dogs get in the RV while I carried in cases of canned vegetables from Costco and other items for the big trip. The dogs had no problem at all adjusting to the RV. It was like a small home on wheels.

The dogs would eagerly get in and find a good spot in a dog bed, on the couch, or just on a blanket on the floor. I'd sit in the RV talking to them or into the camera and record my thoughts. On August 13, 2008, I recorded the following:

"It's been very tiring and very stressful. Stressful having flashbacks. Stressful having memories. Stressful dealing with those memories. It's like a phase you have to go through. You get that it happened. You become aware of it. It has to sink into your body. Then, you have to go through the process of acceptance. Because you want to deny what happened. You don't want to believe it. Then, you learn a little more about how it really has affected your life. You might continue to have flashbacks and memories, but eventually you get to acceptance."

Even though I was still struggling, I decided changing my scenery and taking a trip might be good for me. When the time I planned had arrived, it was August 27, 2008. I had been off work for over three months. I had spoken to Colleen, the human resources director, a few times. While they had approved my short-term disability for two months, at that time they didn't approve any additional time off. I wasn't thinking about the consequences of what would happen if I lost my job. My focus was so intent on trying to cope and survive that I just assumed I would have all the time off work that I needed. I had the impression that the human resource department thought I was well enough to return to work. While I wouldn't have technically had to tell them details about why I was not able to work, I did tell Colleen I was in trauma therapy for sexual abuse.

I suppose on the surface, if one is taking a trip across country in an RV, she might be perceived as being well. I didn't feel as if I was in a position to return to work. I frequently had headaches, and I knew from checking my blood pressure it was extremely high. No matter what, I was convinced a trip to get away would be good for me.

It was a foggy, rainy summer morning, and it had been nearly three years since I had gone to New York City to see *Wicked*, the last memory at the time of when I had done anything for fun. I loaded up my dogs and started out on the first leg of the trip. I backed the long RV out of the driveway and onto the winding country road. I was excited to go on my trip and enjoyed the hypnotic effect of driving. By the time I got to the interstate, I unsafely took the camera out and filmed through the windshield. While the music was playing loudly in the background, I said, "Going on a healing journey, Buddy. Welcome to the RV healing express," as I turned the camera on my beagle who was lying in the front passenger seat curled up in a ball. I was headed to Cape Hatteras, North Carolina. I'm not sure why I picked Cape Hatteras, but I did pick it out of the RV book with various KOA campgrounds listed. Why not? I liked the beach, believed the ocean was healing, and thought it would be cool to camp along the shore in North Carolina. My intention was to spend a week at the beach and then return home.

The first stop was in Hagerstown, Maryland at a KOA campground. It was very close to many battlefields from the Civil War and not too far from Gettysburg, Virginia. Buddy was the official guard dog, as he would stand on the large dashboard and bark at other dogs passing by.

At the campground, the rain finally let up enough for me to

walk the dogs. I stepped out of the RV and took a deep breath as the light rain trickled on my face. I noticed all the beautiful trees surrounding the RV spaces. Just walking in nature gave me a feeling of peace, and that outdoor experience reminded me of the many days I spent with my father walking in the woods.

There were campers of a variety of sizes. I met a woman walking her dog, and we talked about various things. She told me, "Everyone has issues." I assume from those comments I had a very deep conversation with a stranger, which wouldn't have been unusual for me because I had traveled so often and interacted with a wide range of people, frequently engaging in various conversations.

As our trip progressed, the dogs and I found ourselves walking two miles on a hiking trail close to Harper's Ferry, West Virginia. I remember seeing a few backpackers who were making the long trek on the Appalachian Trail, a trip I had always wanted to do but didn't have the time or physical training to complete such a daunting challenge. But two miles? The dogs and I handled that easily.

When our hike was finished, we headed on the road to the Outer Banks in North Carolina. The first leg of the trip took two days. We went through Nags Head, Kill Devil Hills, and finally arrived in Cape Hatteras, our final destination on that leg of the trip.

There was something magical about being on the road. It just put me in a different frame of mind. Additionally, it was a break from multiple days of therapy during the week. In retrospect, the break from such intense therapy did me a world of good. I went from having nearly daily flashbacks to having only two in the nearly three weeks I was away. Although I didn't realize it at the time, I'd say this was a good indicator that the therapy itself was retraumatizing me.

I pulled into the KOA in Cape Hatteras and stopped at the registration desk. I could see the whitecaps of the ocean and smell the salt and seaweed. The kind of distinct, refreshing smells you only get at the beach. It was just about dusk, and the temperature was a pleasant eighty degrees. The light ocean breeze skimmed my cheeks and offered many peaceful gifts from nature.

Fortunately, they had an available space right by the ocean. I felt excited in a good way for the first time in a long time. I was informed there were no dogs allowed on the beach because there was a protected sea turtle area just over the sand dune from my RV space. I was disappointed I couldn't take the dogs on the beach. I had envisioned walking and letting them play in the ocean.

After the first night, I got up in the morning, walked up over the sand dune, and stood with my bare feet in the coarse, grainy sand. It was grounding to take a deep breath, listen to the seagulls squawk, and watch as the ocean's waves crashed the shore and ebbed back slowly into the sea. My head felt calm and serene for the first time in a long time.

When my mother didn't hear from me for a few days, she sent a message to my work email. This came through on my Blackberry, and I didn't know it at the time, but the administrator at work was monitoring my emails. When I responded to my mother that I was at the beach, this gave the impression that I was completely healthy and enjoying a vacation when I should have been at work. This email communication would prove to have dire consequences.

In my last night in North Carolina, I turned on the video camera and said, "*I hope I'm gonna heal. I hope I can get rid of all these memories of sexual abuse. Take it all away and send it out to sea. I want to be in the present moment all the time. That's what my therapist always tells me, "Stay in the present moment." I get it. But what I'm trying to say is I have so many triggers. Even though I conquered a lot of them, knowing I can't be hurt anymore. Now I have memories, and I need to be able to process through each one of them, and it takes a long time. My therapist thinks I can just take a switch and turn them off. I wish I could.*"

Hindsight allows me to see how hard I tried to help myself. One of my own traits that helped me was the ability to focus. While focusing is an excellent trait, fixation, on the other hand, can be detrimental. There were times when I would fixate on a particular memory or obsess over how what happened to me was so wrong. It was a helpless feeling to have no recourse for the damaging effects of sexual assault, and at times I would resist acceptance of that fact. While I carried guilt and shame, a part of me wondered if any of the people who had abused me ever felt an ounce of guilt for what they'd done to me. The sad thing is I doubted they ever thought what they did was wrong.

Once I had opened the doors to my past, closing them became far more difficult than I could have ever imagined. It wasn't as simple as telling myself to "stay in the present moment." I was going to have to overcome my fixations of the memories, and that was a very tall task. I didn't have those insights in the summer of 2008, while I was trudging along my journey as if I was wading through a swamp. Several years later, I would come to understand how to manage those types of thoughts.

~

After being in North Carolina, I impulsively decided to take a trip to Las Vegas while sitting in my RV with the dogs. When I left my home in Pennsylvania, I had only planned on staying at the beach for a week.

I mapped my trip out west from North Carolina because at the time I didn't have GPS. It was September 2008, and I knew the weather would be a little less hot in the desert. I had lived in the west for almost twenty years. I trained at the Olympic Training Center in Colorado Springs and then went on to graduate from college at the University of Arizona in Tucson. I lived in Las Vegas for nearly five years after I graduated from college. I didn't realize it, but thinking back, Las Vegas was a nostalgic place for me. It was a place that held mostly positive memories and where many of my adulthood firsts were accomplished, like first real job, first house, and most importantly, first dog of my own. Chance was rescued from an animal shelter in Las Vegas, and now, fifteen years later, she went back with me and had the opportunity to visit with a good friend.

The trip to Las Vegas from Cape Hatteras was over two thousand miles. I stopped numerous times along the way at various campgrounds and often filmed my experiences. I had many conversations with a wide variety of people. I met the "breakfast club" in McClean, Texas, which was a group of ten women who got together every Saturday to socialize. I filmed them and talked to them for a few minutes.

"So, you are the Breakfast Club?" I asked, knowing the answer because they had told me before I started to film them.

"We are," Vera answered. She had told me her name on camera. "We meet every Saturday to socialize. We don't have a bowling alley or movie theatre or really anywhere to go, so we make our own fun by getting together." I found her comment refreshing, as I believed the connections we make with others are what matters most in life.

"That's really cool," I said in response. I was intrigued by how other people lived and wanted to know more. So, I asked, "You seem to be a group of soulful women and women of faith. Is that right?"

"Oh, yes," many of them answered in unison.

"Well, I think it's awesome you get together like this. Thank you for answering my questions and letting me put you on camera," I said as their breakfast was about to be served.

I filmed a few other things of interest and then got back in the RV and headed back on the road. With all my struggles, all I really wanted was to be mentally healthy and live a peaceful life. I seemed to try to carry on with life to the best of my ability in spite of the circumstances. Certainly, doing things that were outside the norm, but fairly consistent with how I had always lived my life. The only big difference for me was that I was alone with my dogs, and normally I would have been with either family or friends. But being alone wasn't going to stop me from doing what I wanted to do. While it may have seemed impulsive for me to have continued traveling, I was completely aware of what I was doing, and I was staying on schedule with my four medications, and this kept me from having a bipolar episode.

From the time I left home in Pennsylvania all the way out west, it was about ten days since I had a flashback. It was such a peaceful feeling to not be quivering, shaking, and regurgitating traumatic events. Then I got to Holbrook, Arizona, where I was randomly triggered by a man with arms full of tattoos in one of the campgrounds. I felt a sense of danger because he reminded me of a person who scared me when I was a kid. It started with squinting my eyes, followed by my head shaking. I made it back to the RV safely and attempted to get hold of my emotions. While I was crying and shaking, I turned on the video camera and talked about the contents of the flashback. I was battling with the ghosts from my past. While crying into the camera, I said, *"You can't have my present!"* Although I didn't realize it at the time, by speaking into the camera I was assigning words to my memories. I later learned by doing this I was actively transporting the fragmented memory into an integrated place in my brain for storage. At the time, I had limited knowledge of how powerful a tool the video camera had been in helping me to heal, but it proved invaluable.

After around a week of traveling, I finally arrived in Las Vegas. It was sizzling hot with temperatures over one hundred five degrees. I wasn't expecting that kind of heat in September, but it had been a few years since I had been there for a visit. I was so happy to be in a familiar environment that made me feel "normal."

I rented a car and took the dogs for a hike. Even though we walked in the campgrounds where we stopped, it wasn't the same as being on a hiking trail. On the drive to Red Rock Canyon, I remembered how I would take forty or fifty-mile bike rides on the bike paths that ran adjacent to the main road. Once I started therapy in 2005, I had gotten away from doing the things I had once enjoyed. Being in Las Vegas reminded me of what my life was like before my mental health conditions and, specifically, flashbacks started to take a toll on me. I had a wave of disappointment come over me when walking on the trail, as I realized how much my life had been interrupted.

When I first moved to Las Vegas, one of my work colleagues, Nancy, and her husband David kind of looked out for me. They both were at least fifteen years older than I was and made a point of making certain I felt welcomed and cared about. I always knew I could go to Nancy and David for anything. When I adopted Chance from the animal shelter, they kept her for me for two weeks while I moved from an apartment to my house. The last time I saw Nancy and David was during a work conference in 2007. I was able to get in touch with David before I arrived in Las Vegas in the summer of 2008.

When I spoke to David on the phone, he gave me directions to their house and let me know Nancy was out of town. I put the dogs in the rental car and drove about ten miles toward the mountains and above the towering hotel casinos lining the Las

Vegas Strip. David's house was in a beautiful gated community, with lush, green landscaping and a large waterfall at the entrance.

I walked up and rang the doorbell, feeling excited to see an old friend. David opened the door and welcomed me and the dogs. We walked through the house to get to the backyard. He was shocked to see me with my head shaved, because the last time I'd seen him my hair was shoulder length. Even though the hair had begun to grow back about a quarter inch, it was obvious I had shaved my head.

After polite greetings, David asked, "What's going on, Amy? What's happened to you?"

I looked at him and wasn't sure how much detail I wanted to get into. But then I said, "I've been going through a really rough time. I'm in this therapy for sexual abuse that happened years ago, and I can't seem to recover."

"Really?" David seemed concerned but a little shocked. That kind of therapy wasn't exactly a good conversation starter.

"Yeah, it really sucks," I said as I looked over at the dogs roaming toward David's pet turtle he had in his backyard.

"Well, what else have you been doing?" David asked, attempting to change the subject.

"Not much of anything, except trying to survive," I answered, feeling dejected, and realized in that moment of conversation how much my appearance reflected the hell I'd been living through. But it was too much to explain. I didn't even have an explanation at the time for how something that happened decades in the past could be haunting my present. None of it seemed to make sense.

David and I visited for a couple of hours, and then I left and went back to the RV park. I checked my voicemail messages and saw that my mother had called me. When I was in North Carolina, I had spoken to Shelley on the phone. I think more than anything, Shelley and my mom were concerned for my safety. But I wasn't afraid. I was more terrified in my own home having flashbacks than I was in strange places with strange people. At least they were all real and in the present moment.

Driving all those miles, mapping out a place to stay, and taking care of my dogs along the way took a great deal of my energy and focus. These activities forced me to be in the present moment. However, I did have my second flashback one September evening in Las Vegas. I woke up soaking wet with sweat and feeling as if someone had shaken me. It was around two a.m., and I went out to the main area of the RV. I sat down in the kitchen booth and began to tremble. I suspect the flashback was caused by the aftermath of a nightmare. They seemed to go hand in hand. Once I collected myself, I turned on the camera and recorded the following:

"Oh, my God. Really bad memories. Really bad. It is amazing I'm alive. These people who hurt me are, like, really bad. There isn't one of them that I can think of that I'd ever want to see again in my life."

I came to the conclusion that night I needed to chase the ghosts of the past from my head if I was ever going to have mental wellness. I wanted to lay my head on my pillow and sleep like a baby without waking up at all hours of the night shaking and trembling with a feeling of pure terror. After three very long years of suffering, I'm not sure of all the reasons why they stopped, but the flashback in Las Vegas was the last flashback I had until many years later. I had been working very hard to come to terms with my past and move forward with my life.

After those five days in Las Vegas, I decided to make the long journey back home. Instead of taking the southern route through New Mexico, I took a northern route and went through Colorado. Climbing the rugged ridges taxed the RV engine, as it could only go about twenty miles an hour up the steep inclines, eventually getting to Breckenridge, Colorado, where the elevation was about nine thousand feet about sea level. I was elated to get to the top of the mountain and pulled over by a shimmering, blue lake. I had rented a pontoon boat with a group of friends years prior and enjoyed boating on the same lake. It was another reminder of an experience on my pathway that I could feel good about. I reflected on how much joy some of my experiences provided me. I wasn't sad or disappointed. I was hopeful I could experience that kind of joy and happiness again in the future.

I got out of the RV and filmed a storm, with dark clouds and lightning in the distance over the mountain ranges in one direction. The other direction, the sun was shining, making the snow on the mountaintops glisten with a blinding reflection. I took off my hat, looked into the camera, and said, *"Thank God for my healing miracle. I see the dark clouds in the distance, but I choose to go toward the light. It's been a long journey, and sometimes darkness is necessary, but I'd rather walk toward the light."*

I walked slowly back to the RV, breathing the clean, crisp mountain air. I felt a moment of contentment, a feeling that had been eluding me for years. I gained internal strength and was reminded of my resilience while traveling all those miles.

The dogs and I worked our way across the country, stopping at various campgrounds along the way. At one point, I went into a pet store to buy food and treats for the dogs. I rounded the corner of an aisle and came upon a group of women who were handling a beautiful black and white kitten.

"Aww, how cute," I said as I walked up closer to the woman holding the kitten.

"Would you like to hold him?" she asked, motioning me to come closer.

She handed me the kitten and he put his head under my chin. "How old is he? He seems very small," I asked as I pet the kitten.

"He's six weeks old. His mother abandoned him and the entire litter. Would you like to adopt him?" she asked.

"I had been thinking about adopting a cat, but I have three dogs and I'm not sure how he'll get along with them," I commented in response. "They're friendly dogs, so I think they'd be okay with him."

"Well, we only have two kittens left. Let's get you set up to adopt him," she said, and in the moment, I agreed to take him. Perhaps it was another one of my impulsive decisions, but it turned out to be one of the best things about the trip.

When I put the kitten, who I called Mr. Kitty, into the RV, the dogs came over to see what was going on. He wasn't afraid of the dogs and just seemed to fit right in immediately. When we stopped at a campground that had lots of space to walk the dogs off leash, I took Mr. Kitty with us on the walk. And that was how he was trained.

Mr. Kitty turned out to be one of the reasons I kept fighting, even when life seemed to get harder. Just like my dogs, he needed me to take care of him, and I needed him to love.

When I look back, I realize how taking my RV trip allowed me to remember who I was. I had all these accomplishments and adventures in my past that had gotten buried deeply because of the intense focus in therapy on my broken self. In my view, it was one of the fundamental mistakes of both Belinda and Kendra. I believe it's important to take a strength-based approach in a recovery journey. Constantly focusing on what was wrong with me wasn't helping.

In addition, Kendra always told me to "stay in the present moment," but she never taught me or guided me on how to get there, with the exception of a few grounding techniques. Driving a few thousand miles and changing my scenery jolted me back to the present and allowed me to gain additional strength. I didn't know an added bonus to the trip would be for the flashbacks to have ended. Turns out, I got my healing miracle after all.

Chapter 11

After the long trip home, the dogs, Mr. Kitty, and I finally pulled into the parking spot for the RV. I got out and slowly walked into the backyard. My mom had called and left a voicemail for me that a tornado had touched down not too far from my house, and she had gone to check on my house for me. I took one glance at the debris covering the entire backyard and multiple tall oak trees uprooted, breaking the fence and landing partially in my neighbors to the right of my house's backyard. I went from feeling happy and joyous to feeling overwhelmed and a little bit in shock. It was an even bigger mess than my mother had described.

The mess on the outside was an indicator of what the mess on the inside of me was going to become, as I had called Dr. Richard's office for appointments with her and Kendra.

"Hi. This is Amy Gamble, and I need to schedule appointments with both Dr. Richard and Kendra," I said, as one of the first things I did when I returned home was to attempt to take care of my mental health. I had been religiously taking the medications Dr. Richard had prescribed, and I still believed in therapy, even though I'd had some contentious moments with Kendra. I recognized I needed professional help to continue learning how to manage my mental health conditions. As far as I had come, a part of me realized I still had lots of work ahead of me.

In my experience, the receptionist was never known for her friendliness. She bluntly told me, "Amy, you've missed multiple appointments in the past few weeks, and if you miss again, we won't be able to see you anymore."

"Well, I'm sorry, but I've been out of town," I replied, kind of regretting my "throw caution to the wind" attitude, as I now had to come face to face with the reality of where I had left off in my own life.

"This is the last time we are going to overlook these missed appointments. Dr. Richard is very strict about this policy," she said in a kind of bitchy way.

"Okay. I understand," I replied, shrugging as if I didn't care. I was getting really tired and worn down from caring about anything.

When I had my first appointment with Kendra, I slowly walked up the stairs to her office. It was a downer to be going back to therapy, as I had regained a lot of strength on my own during my trip. I wasn't in the mood to revisit my past. I was ready to move forward with our discussions and focus on the present and my future.

Kendra called me back to her office, and I sat down in the chair I always sat in beside her desk. She came in and said, "Amy, you've had a dissociative fugue."

"What's that?" I asked, shocked by her comment and wondering how taking a trip without telling her met the criteria for some other mental health diagnosis.

"That's when you have amnesia, forget who you are, and end up in an unexpected place. You carry on like you're a different person," she said as she looked at me in a shaming kind of way, like I had done something horribly wrong.

"I knew exactly who I was." I pushed back a little but began to feel very insecure. The dynamic with Kendra was one in which she held all the power. I was also not very confident and quickly thrown off balance. "Dissociative fugue?" I questioned where Kendra came up with this idea.

"I told you, Amy, you need to keep yourself safe by staying around your house. Do you understand me?" Kendra said in a more authoritarian kind of way. "You can't miss another appointment. Mm…k?" Kendra said as she kind of glared at me with her piercing, blue eyes. What Kendra didn't understand or realize was I felt better not being isolated in my own home. Even though I had been using multiple coping strategies, such as making the videos, the isolation was doing more harm to my mental health than it was providing a safe haven.

I walked out of that appointment feeling very despondent and disgusted. I wasn't buying the whole idea of having a dissociative fugue. That was total bullshit, and I knew it at the time. Kind of the same theme of creating these stories that matched her own narrative. First my family pulls my hair out at birth, and now just because I took a cross country trip and didn't tell anyone, I've had a rare, dissociative fugue. I finally began to question her competency, though it would take me a couple more years to trust my own judgment.

~

From the end of September until the end of October 2008, I spent the majority of my time cleaning up my backyard. There was no time or energy to create videos, play the piano, or use the drums. I had to clean up all the trees, leaves, and other debris that were in the yard. None of my family came to visit, because I told them I needed space to figure out whether my family was helping me or hurting me. I was still fixated on the hair pulling comment. This left me extremely isolated and now totally reliant on Kendra for emotional support.

By the time December 2008 arrived, I had sunk into a dark, deep depression. The circles around my eyes looked as if someone had given me two black eyes. That marked the beginning of a very long bipolar depressive episode. While the depression was very hard on me, I was dealing head on with the bad memories. I faced my many demons the best way I could with the information I had at the time. But the moving parts that were outside of my control only made the depression worse. All the mixed signals I had given to the human resource department had caught up with me. When the human resources department called, it was my last phone call with them.

"Hi, this is Amy, and you had left a message for me to return your call," I said, a little nervous, wondering what human resources from work wanted to talk about.

"Yes, Amy. How are you doing?" Colleen asked. I'd had a good relationship with Colleen, and she had been somewhat supportive about my journey with sexual abuse therapy, as she had a friend who had gone through something similar.

"Well, I think I'm almost ready to return to work," I replied, wanting to believe I could attempt to return to work in the next few weeks, as the flashbacks had finally stopped after three long years. It turns out my RV trip was the healing trip I had hoped it would be.

"Every time we talk, you say that. I hate to be the one to tell you this, and I'm sorry, Amy, but you're fired," she said rather bluntly. "We'll need you to package up your computer, Blackberry, and all work-related materials and send it back in as soon as you can."

"Fired? What did I do?" I asked, not really sure why I'd been fired.

"Your family medical leave is over, and you haven't returned to work. So, we have no choice but to let you go," Colleen said in a very straightforward way without any emotion. I really had no idea how much time off I had. I wasn't well enough to focus on practical decision making.

"Well, okay. I'll send the stuff back," I said as I sank deeper into the blue lounge chair. I could feel the numbness travel through my entire body. I was shocked. The next thing I remember is unwrapping a piece of chocolate and savoring one moment of a simple pleasure in the middle of my misery.

The point of being out of work was because I was struggling with my mental health. I just didn't have the capacity or mental wellness to function as I normally would have. I believe it was hard for other people to understand what I was going through, in part because it was so complicated. One minute I could be of sound mind and fairly articulate. The next minute I'd struggle with gut-wrenching emotional pain from unwanted, intrusive memories.

I'd never been fired at any job before. I'd always been a high performing employee who often received numerous promotions. Now, I was being fired a week before Christmas. I wondered if firing me was even legal. My thoughts began to race. "This means my career is over. I'll never be able to get another job in this industry, or any other industry, for that matter. Just like I thought, the criminal record will affect me in punishing ways. Oh, my God,

I'm going to lose everything I've worked so hard to achieve."

After I went through my matter of fact thinking, I began to cry. Not a hard cry, just tears falling down my cheeks, nose running, and waves of numbness coming over me. I asked myself, "What have I done to deserve all of this?" And I couldn't come up with one single reason.

By the end of December 2008, I was so depressed I couldn't pick my head up off the pillow. I had little energy to interact with anyone, including my mother. She hadn't been to my house in over four months. I'd sleep into the late afternoon and barely be awake for a couple of hours before going back to bed again. The past had reached up to me so far it pulled me backward. It was like a pair of shark jaws hanging on to me with a relentless grip. Living life in the present moment had become like an exercise in trudging through a dark swamp. I was going to have to come to terms and deal with the fact that my socioeconomic status was going to slowly dwindle, until I had nothing left. The thought of that alone was depressing all by itself.

What I didn't know at the time was for nearly eighteen years my identity was wrapped around my work. I'd had the opportunity to travel all over the country and meet very interesting, intelligent professionals. The material possessions I could live without, but the intellectual stimulation and relationships I had built were going to prove difficult to replace.

I'm not sure why I continued to see Kendra and Dr. Richard during that time. It could have been the fact there were few psychiatrists in the area, or it may have been I just didn't know or understand at that time I could have had other options. Looking back, it's obvious my mental health didn't improve under their care, with the exception of the flashbacks finally ending, but that was probably more of a reflection on my self-help strategies than it was their direct care. I think my trip across the country provided sort of a jolt to my system and helped me focus my energy on something other than my disturbing past. The trip reset me emotionally, as I focused more on positive experiences and grounding activities.

I guess I didn't really know what to expect from treatment. But if working was one of the indicators for quality of care, they failed me. Overall, I felt like a failure, and this type of attitude sank me into even a deeper depression.

Shortly after I found out I was fired, I began to have suicidal thoughts. It was the second time in my life I had ever had to deal with those distressing feelings. The first time I was a sophomore in college and had recently transferred schools. I was around my family and not isolated. This time I was isolated and alone. My faith, dogs, and cat were the only things that provided a protective factor for me and were the main reasons that kept me from taking my own life.

What did I have left to live for? I'd never experienced such unimaginable suffering. It was Christmas 2008, and I kept fighting the battle with suicidal thoughts, and when I came up with a plan, I finally ended up calling 911 and took myself to the psych unit for the second time in six months.

~

I knew the drill at the local community-based psych unit. I sat alone in the cold, bland room on a plastic chair, looking at the stark, bright white walls and familiar dirty carpet, while they looked through a one-way window and observed me. The room checked all the boxes of a stereotypical psych unit room. The only thing I could hear was the buzzing sound of fluorescent lights. Emotionally, I was flooded with guilt, shame, and disappointment.

After they deemed me safe to go to the main unit, I took the long walk with them through the hallways and entered the lockdown unit. I hated that about psych units; it made me feel like I was a prisoner. There's something about not being able to walk out the door that gave me a feeling of claustrophobia, but I needed a safe place to be until I could grasp all the moving parts of my life.

I had been taking four different medications since May 2008 that Dr. Richard had prescribed. But the psychiatrist in the hospital decided I needed all new and different medications. I'm not sure why, and quite frankly, I couldn't have cared less about anything. Depression had that effect on me, draining me of my typical engaged and positive outlook.

I methodically went to the group sessions and listened to

everyone's challenges during the six days I was hospitalized. It was easier to feel sorry for myself when I didn't know or hear about others' stories. Depression didn't steal my empathy away, but it made me lethargic and apathetic.

The day before I was released from the hospital, I was sitting up in my bed and a nurse stood in the entry to the room.

She said, "I know who you are," and she smirked.

"Okay, who am I?" I said in response, shaking my head back and shrugging.

"You're that Olympic athlete from Wheeling, West Virginia. My sister knows all about you," she answered with a smart tone of voice.

"Yep, that's me," I said, not allowing myself to be impacted by her nonverbal hints of shaming me for having mental health challenges. I just really didn't give a shit, though I knew how inappropriate it was for her to say this to me, much less mention how her sister knew me. It was a total privacy violation.

What was I going to do about it? Nothing. A patient in a psych unit is almost always powerless. If I had a complaint, who was going to believe me? Kind of the same situation with psych units as it is with the criminal justice system. Rarely does a person with mental illness have the credibility needed to file any kind of complaint. At that point, all I wanted to do was get out of the hospital and go home.

My mom came to visit me before I was released from the hospital. I had called her when I arrived on the unit to go and look after my dogs. She was always optimistic no matter what the circumstances. She told me, "Everything is going to work out okay. You'll see." I listened but wasn't convinced she was right.

Chapter 12

By January 2009, I had been out of the psych unit for a few days. I had time to think about what I needed to do to take care of myself and my pets. I didn't have to make any rapid decisions, but I could only survive on my own without working for about a year. I had been paying Dr. Richard and Kendra "out of pocket" because they weren't in my insurance company's network. I had to map out a plan of how I was going to keep funding the mental health treatment I was getting. If I only knew then what I know now, I would have without a doubt found new providers, and it probably would have saved me in more ways than one. Without realizing I had other options for my mental health treatment, I stayed in treatment with Kendra and Dr. Richard.

In November 2009, I decided to move to West Virginia to be closer to my family. Even though I had been upset about the hair pulling out comment, I put it all in the back of my mind. It wasn't a resolved issue during that time. More out of necessity, I emotionally stuffed it.

I hadn't lived in West Virginia since I was nineteen years old. I never had the time or reason to revisit or bring to my conscious mind some of the places where the sexual abuse occurred. It was never at the top of my mind until I began therapy in 2005. Although the flashbacks had ended, the aftermath left me raw with emotion. I also had a feeling of complete and utter failure. I had been extremely independent, and now I was about to become dependent on my mother. In four years, I went from living in a multi-million-dollar neighborhood to moving in with my mother in my childhood home in the country. I don't know what would have happened to me if I didn't have family support. I shudder to entertain the possibilities, none of which would have had a positive outcome.

The financial crisis had led to a burst of the housing market and made it impossible at the time for me to sell my house. This led to a financial hardship because I was unable to continue paying the mortgage without my prior income from working, resulting in a foreclosure on my property. I had no choice but to take all the material losses in stride. I didn't like the fact I was losing my material possessions, but I kind of anticipated the outcome.

When I moved to West Virginia, one of the things I had going for me was many people knew me in my hometown from my sports background. In 2004, I had been inducted into a large conference Hall of Fame, and they hung a banner with my name and picture in the local arena. Though I moved to the country, the local town was relatively close by and small, especially compared to some of the places I had lived. I never thought of myself as a high-profile person, but I probably had a bigger profile than I ever acknowledged.

I was still experiencing severe depression, and the last thing I wanted to do was talk to anyone when going out in public. The medications I was taking were prescribed by Dr. Richard, but they weren't really helping with the depression.

By March 2010, after several months of excruciating emotional pain, I climbed out of bed and faced off with the abyss of darkness. I lifted my head full of shoulder length hair as I hopped onto the scale and shockingly realized I was fifty pounds overweight. The medication Dr. Richard had prescribed had caused weight gain, and in combination with depression, it was a wicked combination for putting on unwanted pounds. I was despondent yet determined. On one hand, I didn't want to go out in public and face people who knew me; I felt ashamed of how I looked, and I didn't have an answer for the question, "Where are you working now?" On the other hand, I knew how important it was to go out and engage with others. I asked myself, "What's it gonna be? Overcome this fear and accept myself regardless of what the scale says, or crawl back in bed and keep sleeping until the middle of the afternoon, like I've been doing for months?"

I tucked my pride and my concern about my image away and started going to the gym. One of my former high school basketball coaches had an AAU travel girls' basketball team who I watched practice. I remember a conversation he and I had at the gym one day.

"Amy, it's so good to see you here. I'd like for you to help with the AAU program if you can," said Dr. Gee in a cheerful kind of way.

"I've had a hard time with my mental health. You know I have bipolar disorder, right?" I replied, as blaming all my mental health issues on bipolar disorder was a much easier explanation than getting into the details of what I had been through.

"Amy, kids don't care what you have or what you don't. They only care if you pay attention to them and help them," he responded.

"I never looked at it like that," I said, feeling somewhat hopeful and more normal than I'd felt in a long time.

"The kids would love it if you could help us," Dr. Gee said, reinforcing his point. "Just come to a few practices and see what you think. It would be good for you."

Although the coaching was a volunteer position, the opportunity helped me in so many ways. Anytime I ever thought about disappearing into the woodwork, it always seemed like there was someone there pulling me back into the fray. Shortly after my conversation with Dr. Gee, I started helping him with his AAU club teams. Going to practices and working with the kids gave me a sense of purpose and a reason to get out of bed. Focusing on something positive and outside of myself pushed me forward on my recovery journey at that time.

After working with the AAU team for a few months, many of the parents asked me if I would train their kids either in small groups or individually. I always had a gift in working with and relating to kids, and the parents took notice of my coaching style. I was very competent with technical training and had developed a reputation of being an encouraging coach. I started working with a few kids, and after almost two years, I had trained over two hundred kids and had coached a boys' sixth grade basketball team. I had developed my own small business with the basketball training, and it was relief financially to have some income. Sports and specifically basketball had been such an extremely healthy outlet for me. Giving back and helping young people was one of the most positive memories I had in a very long time.

In the spring of 2010, one of the reasons I was able to push myself and coach was because I had found a local peer support group sponsored by the Depression and Bipolar Support Alliance (DBSA). The meetings were held twice a month. It was a relief to have peers who understood the pain of depression and the loss experienced from debilitating symptoms of mental illness. I had been walking my journey without supports in place, though I did attempt to find a support group when I lived in Pennsylvania. I also continued to see Dr. Richard and Kendra, though the appointments had gone to every three months.

When I went to my first DBSA meeting, I walked in with trepidation. The only thing I knew about DBSA was what I had read on the Internet. I was specifically searching for a support group. I didn't know anyone, and a part of me was relieved no one knew me. What I remember about the group was they were kind, understanding, and encouraging.

In late spring of 2010, I went to a national DBSA conference outside of Chicago. My local chapter leader had suggested I attend. I had the opportunity to listen to a number of speakers, some of whom were authors and business leaders. Though I would never wish my challenges on anyone, it was refreshing to know I was not the only one who had struggled.

After listening to a speaker talk about the intersection between law enforcement and people with mental illness, I walked up to her after her talk was over.

"I just want to let you know I really enjoyed your talk today," I said while thinking about what I was going to ask her.

"Thank you," she replied graciously.

"I had an experience a few years ago when I lived in Arizona and was arrested during a psychotic episode." I kind of blurted it out and slumped my shoulders, as I felt a hint of shame come over me.

"I'm sorry to hear that. It sounds like you weren't having your best day. It's understandable how something like that could happen." I was pleasantly surprised with her response. She was the first person who didn't know me personally who I had told about my experience in Arizona. Speaking to a person who understood mental illness and the sometimes tragic intersection with the criminal justice system was an added bonus.

"No, it wasn't my best day. I'm just wondering if there's any recourse for a person with mental illness who has been wrongfully charged?" I asked.

"Well, how long ago did it happen?"

"A few years ago, in 2006," I said, letting the surreal conversation sink in, as I had not talked about my experience with the police in Arizona. I suppose a part of me thought if I could talk about it, I could stop obsessing over it.

"It seems like it was a difficult experience for you. Sometimes it's best to work through those experiences and put it behind you," she said, and then we were interrupted by another member of the audience.

I nodded and thanked her. I felt a little vulnerable having shared that information with a stranger. But I also noticed I felt a bit of relief. Carrying another secret and being silenced about it only contributed to the amount of guilt and shame I felt. I wasn't ready to go stand on a stage and share my story, but it did give me the courage to share with the members of the DBSA support group. When I explained what happened to me with the police in Arizona, the only feedback I ever received was an overwhelming amount of authentic care and concern for how the lingering memories about that day were affecting me. It took others to point out to me what happened was not my fault before I could begin to believe it myself.

~

In May 2010, I had begun to regain some confidence and get a bit of a breather from depressive symptoms, but some were still lingering. I had started to network with people I had worked with in the past. Billy had his own consulting business in the pharmaceutical industry, and he asked me if I'd like to come and do some work with him. Before I accepted the consulting work, Billy and I had a conversation.

"I need to let you know I had an incident that happened in

Arizona while I was sick," I said in a phone call with Billy.

"What kind of incident?" He seemed interested and wanted to know more.

"I had a psychotic episode and was arrested."

"Was the conviction a felony?"

"No, it was a misdemeanor." I felt so insecure and uncertain when I answered him, not knowing how this conversation was going to turn out.

"As long as it wasn't a felony, you are good."

The moment that phrase came out of his mouth, I realized I had been holding my breath. What my attorney Beth had told me proved to be correct in that instance. It just seemed like I constantly had to figure out how I was going to overcome one obstacle or another. I never even thought about how sharing the fact I had a psychotic episode might sound. I just felt like Billy had a right to know about my past. After our phone call, I was mentally exhausted.

Ironically, one of the first projects I worked on for Billy was creating a depression training module for sales representatives. I sat at my desk and stared at the computer screen, looking at several documents describing the signs, symptoms, and course of depression. It was a strange feeling to identify with having many of those symptoms, though not really an out of body experience because I tended to numb my own personal emotions as I wrote the module. Although I recognized I was still experiencing symptoms of depression.

Things were going fairly well with the consulting work until my black Labrador, Chance, died in August 2010. She was eighteen years old. The grief of losing my beloved dog was so deep it made my depression unbearable. Without being able to concentrate, it made writing almost impossible. I was flooded with so many emotions and memories. My heart ached like I had lost my best friend, because I did. Billy had never owned a pet, so he didn't have a lot of compassion or space for my emotional sadness. He was rightfully focused on the business of completing the project, and I wasn't so sure I was going to be able to deliver on the deadlines. I ended up being able to complete one of the three training modules.

After Chance's death, the only one who experienced more

intense grief than I did was my yellow Labrador, Shasta. She refused to eat, and she was never one to turn down a meal or a treat. I tried everything to stimulate her appetite. She'd take a bite and then tuck her tail between her legs and go lie down. Watching Shasta was like looking in a mirror. I could see the deep sadness in her eyes. No more getting excited about much of anything, and I knew that despondent feeling well.

In November 2010, a few months after Chance died, Shasta died. She was ten years old.

I walked on a trail in the woods a few days later with my beagle, Buddy, and Mr. Kitty trailing behind. The trail was still the same, but two of my faithful companions were gone, leaving me with an empty, hollow feeling. In my prayers, I said, "What do you want from me? I can't take any more," as the salty tears dripped into my mouth when I realized I'd lost something I could never replace. It seemed like the moment I began to trust things were going to get better, something would happen, and my hopes would be shattered.

Chapter 13

The loss of my two dogs sank me into a deep depression, and I ended up quitting the consulting work in November 2010. I reverted to trying to sleep the depression away. Sleeping so much actually tended to make the depression worse, not better. In the winter of 2011, somehow, I managed to return to the gym and start working with young people on their basketball skills. I'm not really sure how I managed to infuse positivity and encouragement while battling depression. Sometimes I think there was so much power in helping someone else that it actually provided a gift to me in the form of relieving my emotional pain.

In November 2011, a major news story broke about one of Penn State football's former coaches, Jerry Sandusky. He was indicted on fifty-two counts of child molestation and was ultimately convicted in June 2012 on forty-five counts of child sexual abuse. The story initially ran constantly in the news cycle. It seemed anytime I turned on the television, I kept hearing about what Jerry Sandusky had done to numerous young people. While watching the news stories, I could feel my stomach churn from anxiety. I was so angry at what Jerry Sandusky did, and it brought out the anger I had inside of me for what one of my high school coaches had done to me.

On November 17, 2011, I brought out the video camera for the first time in a little over a year and recorded the following:

Well, it's been a long journey since I first started videotaping in 2008. It's been a long and arduous recovery. At times I really didn't think I could make it. It's probably been a week now since the Penn State scandal erupted. It's really stirred up a lot of my own feelings about being a victim of sexual abuse and prompted me to take a deep look at whether or not I would actually come forward and report the incidences that occurred and really affected my life in very traumatic ways. I had to make a decision for today that I would not step forward. The best thing I can do is continue to work on my own recovery. I've been a victim, but I don't want to become a villain. Because that's what would happen. People would blame me for what happened, and I can't take being vilified right now.

In 2011, when I made the video, I didn't feel as if I was strong enough to speak up and tell someone in a position of authority what happened with Coach Reynolds. However, after years of watching various high profile sexual assault cases and seeing victims come forward and courageously speak their truth, I had examples to look toward who inspired me to take the first step ten years later and write an email to the local school superintendent.

First, however, I tackled an issue closer to home. In 2021, when I was fifty-six years old and learned Joe was coming into town and would be visiting my mother, I finally had the strength to stand up for myself and speak my truth. I was no longer willing to bear such an incredible burden anymore. I was standing in the kitchen of my mother's house looking out the sliding glass door, contemplating what I was going to say. My mother walked to the edge of the kitchen to see what I was doing. I had a feeling of determination, an inner knowing what I was going to say was coming from a place of inner strength and healing.

"When Joe comes here, I'm leaving. I'm sick and tired of having to pretend nothing happened. He caused me unimaginable pain and sorrow, and I went through hell," I said very pointedly to my mother. I was visibly irritated, no one in my family seemed to consider my experience or feelings.

"I know he did. That's terrible," my mother replied in a very matter of fact manner. I had some inclination that while the conversation we were having was good for me, it might make her feel a bit responsible, even if it had been so many years ago.

"Yes, it was terrible, and it's awful I've been expected to be in the same room with him and pretend as if nothing ever happened. I don't even want to be in the room when you talk about him. I'm done pretending!" I said very sternly and confidently.

"You shouldn't have to pretend," my mother responded, as I imagine some part of her knowing, understanding, and accepting what she had witnessed me going through with all the flashbacks I experienced may have impacted her feelings about it.

"I know you think it was a long time ago, and it has, but what do you think comes into my mind the moment he steps his foot in the door?" I asked my mother, kind of surprised she hadn't thought of these things years earlier.

"You probably think about what he did to you," she said.

I looked at her, a little shocked she acknowledged that, and said, "That's right. And it's not very fun," I stated as I picked up my keys and walked out the door. My parting words were, "I don't care if I ever see Joe again for as long as I live. I'm an adult, and I get to make decisions to take care of myself." As I was leaving, it felt like I grew just a little bit taller.

My mother answered, "You should take care of yourself. I understand."

I stood up for myself, even though it had taken me decades to break through the message of secrecy and the overall minimization of such significantly impactful traumatic events. Research shows sexual abuse takes a toll on mental and physical health, and often these effects don't fully appear until a victim is in adulthood. Similar to other families and our culture in general, my family underestimated and downplayed the damaging effects of sexual abuse on me.

One of the conflicting thoughts I had to deal with about Mr. Brock was he was a friend of my grandfather. One of the conflicting thoughts about Joe was he was a family member and almost everyone liked him.

I liked Joe. He was funny and always seemed to be laughing about something. He was an auto mechanic and always had endless dirt and grime under his fingernails and stained on his hands. It used to make me cringe to see someone with grease on their hands. I never knew why until I painstakingly processed the sexual abuse memories alone and in therapy. Now, it doesn't bother me anymore except sometimes it reminds me of Joe, and even though I'd like to forget all the trauma he inflicted upon me, the mentioning of his name takes me back to the day in my grandfather's mildewed basement when Joe's acts escalated.

The level of internal conflict I had about Joe and Mr. Brock being either evil or good later became the same kind of internal conflict I'd have about my high school coach. On one hand, he helped build my confidence with the countless hours he would spend talking to me about other "blue chip" athletes he knew or had grown up with. They were all male athletes, but it didn't matter. Their path to elite athleticism was what mattered to me. There's no question I enjoyed the support and encouragement, and it really helped me. On the other hand, he was manipulating me with conversations about how I should look, how much I should weigh, and who I should be friends with.

One of the reasons I didn't tell my mother about what happened to me with my coach was because I felt like it was my fault. The other reason was the prior sexual abuse was not talked about much. Like many families, our family had plenty of secrets. Sexual abuse is one of those taboo topics my family never wanted to discuss, not so different than other families where this has occurred. My mother never told my father about the sexual abuse I experienced. I'm not sure why. I do remember her telling me not to tell my father. Holding my secret meant as a child I had to bear the burden of holding on to and processing these traumatic experiences, all the while trying to overcome the intense amount of shame I felt.

~

During 2021, I had been driving by the high school much more frequently, and I realized I'd feel emotionally numb anytime I drove by and saw the entrance to the auditorium. I was remembering with greater frequency that tragic day when I became a sexual abuse victim for the fourth time in my life. My awareness level of how I felt had increased substantially from using mindfulness strategies and being keenly aware of how I felt in my body. By that point, I had many strategies to stay in the present moment and feel my emotions in real time.

I had become frustrated the past was showing up in my present. I also received a letter from the high school athletic director telling me they were inducting me into my high school athletic

Hall of Fame. They were also inducting coaches, and though I'm unsure if my coach would have been nominated, I didn't think it was right for a coach who had abused me and potentially other students to be inducted into the Hall of Fame and be celebrated for his accomplishments as a coach. More than anything, I wanted to know what the school system was doing to protect students and athletes from predatory teachers and coaches. I was motivated by my desire to make sure I could do everything in my power to assure potential students didn't become victims of sexual abuse. I wanted to raise the level of awareness that this type of abuse did occur and point out how unacceptable it was and is for this to happen.

I knew the local superintendent of schools because I had done multiple mental health trainings for the school system, including some in the very auditorium where the sexual assault had occurred.

I sat at my desk and formulated what I wanted to say. I outlined in my email how I was sexually assaulted by my high school coach in the school auditorium. I then went on to ask the superintendent what protections were in place for current students. When I pressed send on that email, I had a sense of empowerment and could feel my inner strength come to the forefront.

It's not easy to speak up about sexual assault for a multitude of reasons, however, the year 2021 was my turning point to hold my ground. It began by choosing not to ever see Joe again. It continued when the superintendent invited me to come to her office and speak with her.

It was a beautiful early fall day in West Virginia. As I drove to the county school office, I felt internally strong, somewhat relieved, and a bit nervous. After decades of holding on to a horrible secret, I finally had the opportunity to disclose the heavy burden I'd been carrying with me for years. It was a time in my healing journey to move from being a victim to being a survivor who was learning to thrive.

I walked into the county office and let them know I had an appointment with Tammy, the superintendent of schools. I was calm, but a little nervous thinking about how I was going to articulate what happened to me.

Tammy approached me and invited me to follow her to a small conference room. We had polite chit chat and then sat down around the table.

Tammy said, "Amy, before you say anything, we could just go to lunch as friends and have a conversation. But once you start talking in this building I have to put on my administrative hat and act in my role as superintendent of schools." I looked at her and pondered why she was saying this to me.

"No, that's okay. I'd rather have this conversation here." I'd come this far with self-disclosure, and I wasn't going to be deterred any longer from speaking my truth.

"I'm really worried about you, Amy," Tammy said, raising her brow and genuinely looking concerned for me.

"Are you worried because of what people may think if I come forward publicly?" I asked, somewhat confused, but wondering what she was actually worried about.

I don't remember what she said in response to my question. My mind was swimming with thoughts.

Then, the words just started flowing right out of me.

"There were several incidents of sexual assault that occurred by Coach Reynolds, and often there was alcohol involved," I said, speaking with a passionate purpose while giving my unfortunate experiences a name.

"Why do athletes always get involved in so much drinking behavior?" Tammy asked and clearly diverted the conversation away from the assaults.

"I don't know. It was probably part of the culture." I attempted to bring the conversation back to talking about the abuse. "I realize what I'm telling you happened a long time ago, but I just don't think it's right for a coach to ever be considered for the Hall of Fame. I needed to let you know what happened, because it wasn't right," I said, feeling more empowered with each statement I made.

It seemed to me Tammy attempted to minimize the sexual abuse. In fairness to Tammy, the abuse happened many years prior. But she did listen to my story and assured me they were doing everything they could to prevent this from happening to other students.

As for the Hall of Fame, Tammy said, "I can't keep him from

getting inducted to the Hall of Fame because there were never any criminal charges filed." I nodded in understanding, though I was disappointed in her response.

Coach Reynolds hadn't worked in the school system for several years, so there wasn't any way to directly address the situation with him. Although there is no statute of limitation in the state of West Virginia for reporting sexual assaults, I personally didn't want to go down that pathway. Mostly because I didn't want to think about that abuse any more than I had to, and I for sure didn't want to have to relive it ever again.

On that fall day in 2021, I was so relieved when I walked out of that office. In the moment, it really sank in why it's so hard to report sexual assault. I can't even imagine how difficult it would be if I were a teenager coming forward. The gravity of the situation is so heavy, literally and figuratively speaking. I didn't think about it at the time, but it probably would have been helpful for me to have an advocate with me. Someone who I could know without a shadow of a doubt would be there to support me. Instead, I went on my own, and I was proud of myself for revealing the abuse and speaking truth to power. It didn't matter it happened decades ago. Having the opportunity to be heard was invaluable.

Although Tammy did a bit of blaming the victim, I knew none of the sexual assault I had experienced was my fault. The coach was an adult who knew better and should have been someone I could trust. Instead, he was nothing more than a perpetrator disguised as a teacher and coach. Even though I have regrets about drinking alcohol, I recognize a responsible adult would never have sexually exploited a student-athlete. What the coach did to me was illegal, unethical, and contributed to causing significant challenges for me with my mental health.

Even though the sexual assault by my coach occurred decades ago, there are very few days when I drive by the high school and don't think about what happened in that auditorium. It's not something I want to remember, but it's not like I can press a delete key and eliminate the memory. I've integrated the traumatic memory and have mostly healed from the consequences and aftermath. But there are still some days when I wish the past would stay dormant and not show up uninvited in my present.

When I could finally talk about my experiences with sexual assault, I realized on some level my struggles with suicidal thoughts were a direct result of dealing with reliving the traumatic events through memories and flashbacks. Childhood sexual abuse has been consistently associated with suicidal behavior. It's hard to describe the intense emotional burden of being a victim. Depression, guilt, flashbacks, shame, fear, and anxiety, to name a few, are all very common responses to sexual assault.

Over the years and up until that point, I battled back and refused to be defeated. I frequently talked in my videos about how my abusers were not going to "win," because I believed in the message that in the end "the good guys always win!" While that's not always the case, in my situation believing it inspired me to keep fighting even when my suffering made me feel like giving up. I've come to realize that once I could give the abuse a name and make sense of how it affected me, in time the traumatic events lost their power over me and I had a sense of peace.

~

However, in 2011, I'd not yet resolved the trauma, and the Penn State scandal brought up unresolved traumatic experiences. Some I had processed through in therapy with Kendra, and other memories were coming to the forefront of my mind. Even though I had relocated to West Virginia, I had continued to see Dr. Richard and Kendra. I would make the ninety-minute drive for my once every three months appointment. Hearing about Jerry Sandusky had triggered a reemergence and flood of disturbing memories, and while I didn't experience flashbacks, I did have to process many emotions. I had gotten to a point where my memories were integrated, which meant I could put them into a narrative context. The memories had words with meaning. But I still had an overwhelming feeling of fright. It was always easier to deal with things when it was a trickling amount of information and not a flood.

By January 2012, I was also frustrated with the weight gain I had experienced from an anti-psychotic medication I was taking. It was a sublingual pill that would dissolve under my tongue, and within minutes it would stimulate a raging hunger.

I sat in Dr. Richard's office and asked, "Can I stop taking Saphris? It's really causing a lot of weight gain, and I'm worried about getting high cholesterol and diabetes." I knew from my days in the pharmaceutical industry of the many side effects from anti-psychotic medications. I hadn't considered the effects of abruptly stopping the medication. I didn't know at the time how important it was for me to take an anti-psychotic for bipolar disorder to prevent a psychotic episode from occurring.

"If you want to stop taking it, that's okay," Dr. Richard replied without offering any alternative medications. In my experience, when I saw Dr. Richard, I was generally the one who asked for various medications. I initially asked for an anti-psychotic because I knew I needed one to help clear my thoughts and cope with symptoms. Anti-psychotics have many uses and are often prescribed for people who live with bipolar disorder.

And that conversation and subsequent stopping of a crucial class of drugs that kept me mentally healthy at the time would prove to have dreadful consequences. Even with my background in the pharmaceutical industry, I didn't have the same type of understanding about my mental health conditions in 2012 as I do today. I had to become a student of how the many symptoms I experienced affected me and how I needed to manage them.

By the fall of 2012, I began to experience hypomania. I hadn't noticed any difference in the effects of not taking Saphris earlier in the year, but later realized the shift in mood was occurring gradually. The symptoms would first show up with interrupted sleep. Lack of sleep would supercharge the hypomania, and then a few hours' reduction in sleep turned into sleeping for a couple of hours a night. Lack of sleep for a day or two didn't affect me, but it was the cumulative effects of going days without sleeping very much.

I was no longer training kids in basketball and had finished my coaching responsibilities. I had hoped to return to the pharmaceutical industry as a consultant, so, I voluntarily dissolved my basketball training business. This left me without structure in my days. Structure often provided motivation to have proper self-care, like sleeping an adequate number of hours a night.

My stress level was fairly high because I was worried about

what my future would look like. I needed a sense of purpose to stay motivated. I enrolled and was accepted into a doctoral program in organizational leadership. At the time, I believed if I had additional education, I may be able to return to the pharmaceutical industry as a consultant.

Because I was videotaping and taking pictures during this timeframe, I can see that I was stressed for a number of reasons. One external stressor was when a household oil tank ruptured and sent an abundance of heating oil into my basement. This left me with a high level of anxiety which, in retrospect, probably triggered symptoms of mania. The way I understood how bipolar disorder affected me is high levels of mania would lead to psychosis.

The final breaking point came when I was entertaining my nephew, Tony, and he was playing with Play-Doh the way eight-year-old boys do. As we sat at the kitchen table with the Play-Doh on top of newspapers, Tony proceeded to give all of his figures private parts. The pungent smell of Play-Doh wafting up my nose made my eyes water. I squeezed my eyes closed and could feel a wave of numbness come over me. The Play-Doh was something I played with frequently as a kid. Tony was at the age when some of my sexual abuse took place, and that made me really sensitive to my past traumas.

After Tony went home, I packaged up the figures he made and put them in a box. I had planned to show them to my niece Natalie and explain to her what I was concerned about. I remember having this overwhelming feeling of fear, believing someone was hurting Tony and someone was trying to hurt me, and those paranoid thoughts escalated quickly into believing my family was trying to poison me.

At the end of October 2012, about two days after playing with Tony, I called Dr. Richard's office.

"I need to make an appointment with Dr. Richard. Something just isn't right," I said to the receptionist.

"You were just here in September, Amy. Why do you need to see her now?" the receptionist asked with a hint of frustration.

"I'm really struggling, and I don't know what's wrong with me," I answered, stumbling over some of my words and feeling more paranoid with every minute passing.

"Dr. Richard can't see you for two weeks," she bluntly stated.

"Well, okay. I'll take the two-week appointment, I guess."

I hung up the phone and could feel a wave of disappointment. Paranoid thoughts were popping into my head. I was obsessing over the thought of someone hurting Tony. My stress response was causing an increase in anxiety, and I wasn't able to articulate the specifics of what was happening to me.

Chapter 14

In early November 2012, a week before I was supposed to see Dr. Richards, I woke up early in the morning, packed a bag, and threw it in the back of my Chevrolet Avalanche, a full-size pick-up truck with four-wheel drive. I was amped up with anxiety, having feelings of terror and so delusional I couldn't think straight. The fear of someone hurting me was haunting my psyche. My mind was tormented with repetitive thoughts of my family trying to kill me. I wasn't able to discern the difference between a false thought and a thought based in reality.

Even though in my present circumstances I was safe, the stress response I experienced when I falsely believed someone was hurting me triggered mania. The symptoms of bipolar disorder and PTSD were erupting, and I didn't know I was sick. It was six years since I'd had a psychotic episode in Arizona. I had lost all insight into my condition, making me extraordinarily vulnerable.

I began driving west. I don't know why, except driving seemed to be a calming activity. Looking back, it was remarkable to think how my brain could be aware enough to drive a motor vehicle, but not aware enough to know I was sick.

I ended up stopping in Indiana, which was about seven hours from my home in West Virginia. I remember driving to a convenience store and parking in front. I fell asleep for a short time. When I woke up, I had a moment of knowing something was wrong. I took myself to a hospital emergency room and told them something wasn't quite right with me. Even though I was struggling with my thoughts, I had an intuitive feeling that I was mentally unwell. But I wasn't able to articulate what was running through my mind. They took some x-rays and released me with a prescription for a heartburn medication.

After leaving the hospital, I got back on the road again and started driving north. I have no idea why I picked that direction. My thoughts were completely out of touch with reality. I was convinced I could communicate with a variety of famous people. At one point, I rolled down my window and began talking out loud, as if they were really able to hear me. I pleaded with them to help save children who were being abused.

Racing thoughts have a way of randomly jumping from one topic to the next. There was the overwhelming thought of my family trying to poison me, which triggered a stress response, making my thoughts swirl in my mind. I would equate the experience of psychosis with waking up from a dream when your thoughts aren't totally aware of where you are. It's kind of an altered state, which lasts for a few moments, until you realize you've been dreaming. In my experience, I've come back to reality quickly after receiving the right medications. However, since I'd stopped taking the Saphris with no replacement, my thoughts continued to spiral. Acting on those thoughts was literally taking me down a dangerous pathway.

I drove into the early hours of the morning and finally ran out of gas on a highway in Northern Michigan close to the Canadian border. The vehicle slowly drifted into a guardrail and came to a stop. I sat there and dozed off.

Right about sunrise, another motorist stopped to ask me if I was okay. I said, "No. I need help," not really sure what kind of help I needed, but enough awareness to ask for help. The kind man called 911, and an emergency rescue team showed up to take care of me.

They took me out of the Avalanche and laid me down on a stretcher in the back of the ambulance. My body began to shake uncontrollably, as if I was convulsing. An indescribable level of fear was overtaking me. The emergency rescue team thought I was having a seizure, but I was experiencing violent flashbacks for the first time in four years. The same repetitive flashback I'd experienced in the Arizona desert. It was like I was in the grass all over again. Helpless. The more the EMTs tried to control my body, the more intense the feelings of terror. Everything seemed heightened and distorted, creating a profound sense of vulnerability and powerlessness. They put a neck brace on me and took me to the small community hospital in a rural part of Michigan.

No one from my family knew where I had gone, but they knew I was missing. The local sheriff found my identification in the vehicle and called my mother. She told them I had bipolar disorder and was in need of psychiatric help. There was a lack of understanding about trauma by my family and in general a dismissal of my severe symptoms of PTSD. It was always easier for my family to place blame on me for not managing bipolar disorder correctly.

All of my immediate family and I had multiple experiences with my mom and sister, Sherry, having psychotic episodes at one time or another. It's exhausting for loved ones to deal with someone with untreated or undertreated mental illness.

My family, in general, had a tendency to blame me when I experienced severe symptoms. In the throes of a psychotic episode, it wasn't helpful to sternly say in a patronizing manner, "Just take your medicine!" Though not taking an anti-psychotic medication was a dangerous risk. Without Dr. Richard explaining to me what might happen if I didn't take the medication, I had no idea I was at high risk for having a psychotic break.

The high stress from a triggering event, like the Jerry Sandusky case, brought to the forefront unresolved past traumas and led to an increase in mania. The enormous amount of stress I experienced led to a psychotic break. The fact that I had been actively seeking mental health treatment from Dr. Richard and Kendra got lost in the dramatic intensity of my decompensated mental health state.

What I didn't know years ago is that a psychotic episode can occur with PTSD and childhood sexual abuse involving rape prior to sixteen years of age, and is strongly associated with psychosis. In my case, it was probably a combination of reemergent trauma memories and bipolar disorder that caused the break. Clearly, the fallout from lack of quality mental health treatment had once again caught up with me.

In the hospital, they decided to transport me by ambulance to a city with a psych unit two hours away. The EMTs led me into the back of the ambulance, and I sat down on a stretcher. I was very calm and relatively coherent. Two EMTs took duct tape, placed it directly on my skin, and restrained my hands and feet to the metal parts of the ambulance stretcher. I don't know why they restrained me, other than they knew I was a mental health patient. The triggering effect of feeling I was in danger and couldn't move transported my mind back in time to a place where I was held against my will. My pulse went through the roof, my blood pressure rocketed, and my mind dissipated into a world of multiple falsehoods. I began to believe the EMTs were taking me to an underground place where they would harvest my organs. It was the longest two-hour ride I have ever experienced in my life. Eventually, I ended up in a psych unit where they attempted to treat me with medications.

I sat in one of the large common rooms and used the payphone to call my mother. "They're trying to harvest my organs, and I'm really scared," I said to my mother as quietly as possible so the staff couldn't hear me.

"No one is trying to hurt you, Amy. Take your medicine. You need your medicine." Though she was kind about it, my mom continued to repeat the same phrase.

Though my mom had good intentions of reinforcing the necessity of having the right medication, I wasn't in the position mentally to understand what she was telling me. When I experienced psychotic symptoms, it was very difficult to comprehend there was a reality that was different than what my thoughts were telling me. The mental strain I experienced made it difficult to relax or find a moment of peace. I was in a relentless cycle of constant stress hormones, like cortisol and adrenaline being released into my system. They were having a direct effect on my physical well-being, interrupting my sleep, and decreasing my appetite. Mental health and physical health are intertwined.

In the Michigan hospital, most of the time I refused the medications they attempted to give me because I thought they were trying to poison me. It's against the law to force medications, even if the doctors know the person can benefit from them. Looking back, I don't think the mental health care providers did a very good job of assessing me.

For the most part, I remember the staff were very kind and caring. I did give the hospital Dr. Richard's contact information, and I believe they called her. If she provided any feedback, I don't think her insight into my condition was helpful. After years of my own education about bipolar disorder and PTSD, I don't believe she was a very competent psychiatrist.

When I was released from the hospital, Shelley and my mom came to pick me up from the psych unit. One thing I know for sure is that I wasn't stabilized on medications, and I was still experiencing symptoms of psychosis. The fire chief had stored my Avalanche in the fire department, so we picked it up on the way out of town. On the drive home, every headlight that shined in the rearview mirror, I thought was a person who was following us in an attempt to kidnap and hurt us.

It was the end of November 2012, and I'd only been home from the hospital for a few days. I woke up in the middle of the night and left my home again. I was experiencing delusions to the point where I had lost almost all touch with reality. One racing thought after another of someone hurting me and hurting Tony.

Once again, I drove west. This time I headed toward New Mexico, only stopping for gas along the way. I had taken a box of Saphris with me that was left over from what Dr. Richards had prescribed. When I stopped at a hotel in Albuquerque, I took one of the pills. The first time I'd taken one since early January 2012. I think some part of me knew I wasn't well. After taking a shower, I lay down in the bed to sleep. Moments after I closed my eyes, a group of boys pounded on my door and scared me. I immediately packed my bag and took off on the road again.

This time I drove north toward Colorado. I had lived in Colorado Springs during my time training for the Olympics, so it was another familiar place to me. My thoughts were all over the board. I began to have a prevailing thought that I was a rogue FBI agent, and the government was trying to track me down. When I saw the white sands in the desert, I thought the government was testing a nuclear bomb without telling the public what they were doing. One of the worst vulnerable positions I'd found myself in.

When I got to Colorado Springs, I think the medication I'd taken in Albuquerque began to take effect because I called my mother. I wouldn't have called her if I was still paranoid about my family poisoning me. The medication probably helped clear my head, if only temporarily. The great benefit I had was that I responded to medication quite rapidly. But at the time I didn't have a therapeutic level of medication in my system. One pill was not enough to bring me back to reality.

"Amy? Where are you?" my mother asked with lots of concern in her voice.

"I'm in Pennsylvania. I'll be home soon," I answered, lying to her because I didn't want her to worry about me.

"We're worried about you. I think you should come home now!" she said with a genuine caring tone of voice distinct to only a mother.

"I'll be home soon. I gotta go. I'll talk to you later," I said and quickly hung up the phone.

In a fleeting thought, I had considered asking her to fly to Colorado and drive me home. I'm not sure why I didn't tell her the truth, but I think a part of me didn't want her to worry about me any more than she already was. One thing about my immediate family was no matter how difficult the situation or circumstance, we never turned our back on one another. It didn't matter if it was a stigmatized mental illness that led to overtly dramatic situations and over the top worry. We always stood by each other.

After speaking to my mom, the next morning I began driving north and then west. I didn't really know where I was going. I stopped to get gas outside of Missoula, Montana, and purchased a bundle of wood. One of my random thoughts was I had planned to camp somewhere. Though it made no sense to camp in the freezing cold with temperatures in the teens, and without the proper supplies and equipment. But I wasn't thinking rationally.

Eventually, I ended up taking an exit for a small town in the western part of Montana about two hours east of Coeur d'Alene, Idaho. It was late afternoon as I drove off the exit on a country road and kept driving until the road came to an end, where a large log cabin sat tucked away all by itself in the mountains. There was a small studio apartment detached and separate from the main house. There was a swing set with three swings, an outdoor garage with a small truck parked inside, and an outdoor deck off the kitchen area. There was an open space in the backyard. It was significantly large.

There was over a half of foot of snow on the ground, the temperature was below freezing, and the snow was trickling out of the sky. As I pulled into the backyard, I believed the log cabin was mine and my friends were waiting in the basement to throw me a birthday party.

I walked up to the back door, turned the unlocked handle, and opened it. I went into the cabin and made myself a cup of coffee, built a fire, watched *The Simpsons* on television, and pretty much made myself at home. Shortly after being inside, I went outside into the backyard and took a bundle of wood out of the back of my Avalanche and built a fire in the open space.

When I opened the Avalanche door, an extra dog tag I had made for Buddy the beagle with my name and phone number on it fell out and landed next to the fire I had built. I wasn't aware the dog tag fell out. I was pacing back and forth and randomly taking items out of the Avalanche and throwing them in the fire, including a sleeping bag, iPad, and cell phone. I thought the government was tracking me, so I disabled the GPS system on the Avalanche.

As for the fire, if I were thinking clearly, I'd say I built a fire so I could stay warm outside. Building outdoor campfires in the woods was something I did frequently. In my right mind, I would never build a fire in someone's backyard. There was no logical reason I would have done something like this.

After being at the cabin for a few hours, I decided if I was going to stay there for the winter, I'd need to go get supplies. I got in my vehicle and started driving west again. It had taken me several days to drive over three thousand miles. It was the first week of December 2012, and the temperature was seventeen degrees and snowing. The snow was coming down so hard I could barely see through the windshield. I kept driving and driving until I crossed the Idaho state line and took the exit for the Idaho National Forest.

At this point, my many delusions were running rampant in my head, and I began to hear voices, something that had never happened to me before that point. I thought two friends were in the vehicle with me and were yelling at me.

"Stop yelling at me," I said as I looked at the passenger seat, convinced my friend Perry was sitting there. I was holding my head in my hands and trying to make the voices stop.

"I'm not yelling at you. I just want you to stop driving," the voice in my head said, as if Perry was talking directly to me.

In my mind, I heard another voice. "You don't know where you're going. It's getting dark, and you got us lost."

"Get out!" I yelled and stopped and opened the door as if I was letting real people out. It was beyond the worst mental state I'd found myself in. After I physically opened the doors and got back in the Avalanche, the voices stopped.

I kept driving deeper and deeper into the backcountry, eventually getting to a service vehicle road. The road had a wooden bar across it, blocking the entrance. I drove through and broke the bar. It was a narrow road that had no vehicle tracks in the snow. The many tall trees were close to the shoulder of the road. I drove in about a foot of snow until I ran over a large, downed tree, puncturing the tire, and I was forced to stop. It was pitch black outside and snowing. I was wearing nylon sweats, a sweatshirt with a nylon jacket, and a pair of moccasin boots without socks. No gloves, no coat, and no hat. I stepped out of the vehicle and began walking deeper and deeper into the forest.

There was no rational reason I left the road and began walking in the forest. I was disoriented and had no idea where I was walking. The snow plummeted from the sky and relentlessly fell against my face, catching on my eyelashes and melting into my eyes. The water-colored blurriness made it difficult to see in front of me. I didn't notice how cold it was outside, but it was well below freezing. It was so quiet on the outside, but in my mind, it was noisy with relentless random thoughts of the government tracking me so they could kill me and the overwhelming belief they controlled the weather. Very often I would walk into areas with a thick abundance of trees, which provided a canopy overhead. I believed the trees would make it impossible to find me even with the chip that was implanted into my body.

As the hours slipped by, the darkness gave way to the sunrise, and the snow stopped falling. I began to have thoughts of how I was going to find my way out of the forest. The tall evergreen trees were so close together I couldn't see where they ended. I was standing at the bottom of a valley where a fairly wide, rushing stream temporarily deterred me from walking any farther. I turned around and attempted to retrace my steps and go back up the mountain. The realization of needing to find my way back to the Avalanche was beginning to pop into my mind. I hadn't begun to panic, but I did make a point of putting my hands into the pockets of my jacket. A natural reaction to protecting my hands from the elements.

Finally, when the dark night came, I found a place under a tree where there was no snow on the ground. I lay down in utter exhaustion. I don't know how many miles I had traveled in over twenty-four hours straight of walking. The only other living being I saw was one deer.

I slept for a little while until the rain began to pour. The good news was the temperature had ticked up above freezing, which was probably a good thing. I saw my tracks in the snow and tried to walk in that direction, but the snow was so deep I couldn't manage to plunge through it. I couldn't feel the weakness in my body or the lightheadedness that would have come from being dehydrated from not having anything to eat or drink, especially after expending so much energy. I turned around and walked back down into the valley.

As I walked back up the mountain on some sort of road, I stopped and said out loud, "Oh, my God, I'm mentally ill. Oh, my God, I'm lost." For a moment, I panicked. I stopped walking and looked around, and all I could see were endless tall trees. I began to pray out loud. "God, help me. I'm so sick. Please, you gotta help. I don't wanna die." I had an intense feeling of regret. I stood there in disbelief. It was like I had woken up from a bad nightmare. It's somewhat inexplicable why all of a sudden I came back to reality.

Because I was an avid hiker, it really sank in when I realized I was lost. I experienced an unimaginable fear. An intense moment of complete helplessness, despair, and desperation. I was shocked and petrified when I picked up my head and finally took in my surroundings. It was as if I had been transported there and was adjusting to the environment. I noticed the forest was stunning in its beauty and vastly dangerous for a lone hiker without the proper boots, clothing, and water. It was a striking moment of mental clarity that most likely saved my life.

I quickly reverted into survival mode, attempting to think my way out of the predicament I found myself in. At last, my mind was no longer working against me, but rather it had become a great asset to my survival. The other asset I had was my natural physical strength and stamina. I was blessed to have my mind and body working together. I also had a wobbly but unwavering faith that God was on my side. My mother always told me I had a guardian angel looking out for me. Perhaps she was right.

When my survival instincts kicked in, I realized I had to keep moving to maintain my body temperature. I had some awareness of what hypothermia would do, and the fear of dying was driving me to survive in every way possible. There I was, standing with my feet numb, my clothes soaking wet, and my legs chafed with blisters on their way to becoming wounds.

Because of my experience of being a hiker and an experienced backpacker, I'd been in the forest on those occasions before. Coming back to reality, I knew from my past experiences that I was not equipped in any way to be this deep in the forest all alone and without any equipment or supplies. After days of having zero awareness of my body's needs, all of a sudden I could finally feel hungry, thirsty, and lonely. An aching loneliness that made me wish for the comfort of my safe, warm home, surrounded by the people who loved me. I feared I would never see any of them again. I didn't shed many tears, but my eyes watered as I thought about the complicated situation I'd gotten myself into.

After feeling the fear, I shifted into my task-oriented, determined self. I walked and I walked, singing a variety of songs out loud to keep myself occupied and eliminate the deafening silence of the wilderness. I finally collapsed on the side of a dirt road. I lay down, thought I wasn't going to wake up, and said out loud, "God, forgive me. I'm sorry. I hope my mom knows I love her." And then I closed my eyes and fell asleep.

Lying by the side of the road, I don't know where it came from or really what it was, but I felt an electric jolt run through my body. It woke me up, and I immediately got up and started walking again. Over and over in my mind, I kept saying, "Keep walking."

I wandered down toward the stream, and this time I decided to cross it. I took a large stick to determine how deep the water was, as I knew enough to not want to submerge my body in freezing cold water. But this meant my feet and my shins up to my knees were now submerged in ice cold water. I was soaking wet, and my toes were well on their way to being frostbitten.

After crossing the stream, I used the large stick as a walking stick and traipsed up the mountain in a place where it had been timbered. Sometimes it was so steep I had to get down on my hands and knees and crawl. I was hanging on to the timbered evergreen trees and climbing over each one of them like I was mounting a horse. Sometimes my flimsy boots would slip, and I would fall face down in the dirt. At one point, I was so hungry I ate leaves.

As I fell and sat on the cold ground in the snow, I glanced around and had a moment of taking in all the beauty nature had to offer. My goal was to get to the top of the mountain, in hopes I could see what direction to walk in, with the mission of finding another human being.

When I got to what I thought was the top of the mountain, I realized it was an incline with a leveling off point. It seemed like there were even more trees that I couldn't see around. I felt like the mountain was going to swallow me up. I was like a needle in a haystack. Even if someone were trying to find me, it would have been extremely difficult. But no one even knew where I was. I was fighting the thought of "why bother," with the countering thought of "don't you dare give up!"

I felt defeated when my plan to find civilization didn't pan out. I decided to walk back down the mountain, and when I did, I came upon a small waterfall that led into another smaller stream. I followed it down the side of the mountain and drank from the stream. It was the first time I had anything to drink in nearly three days. The water helped calm the hunger pangs.

Even though I was sliding and slipping alongside the waterfall, I was driven to get back down the mountain. Because of the rain, my clothes were drenched and heavy with water. I had a sick feeling that I wasn't going to make it through the night unless I found someone to help me. The daunting fear of death was driving me to keep moving.

When I finally got back down the mountain, in the distance, I could hear an engine of what sounded like an ATV. It seemed to be fairly close. The relief and desperate sensation of believing I was going to be saved washed over me and drove me to walk as fast as I could with numb, frostbitten feet. I tried to run toward the engine noise, but the nerve pain shot up my legs and caused significant discomfort. When the engine stopped, I had a wave of relief flow through my body. I thought, "Someone is going to help me."

I walked up on the couple, and they were very startled to see me. I found out later they were brother and sister out enjoying the backcountry for the day. They had planned to build an outdoor fire and warm up before going back up the trail and calling it quits for the day.

"Help me, please!" I pleaded with a raspy, dehydrated voice. Begging them to help me. I had a feeling of tremendous relief. A calm and peaceful sensation that came in waves.

"Are you alone?" the startled woman asked.

"Yes, I'm alone, and I'm lost," I answered, feeling relieved and intuitively grateful to see two approachable strangers.

"What's your name?" she asked as she put her hands on my cheeks and held my head in place.

"I'm Amy Gamble," I answered.

"Where's your vehicle?" she asked, as if confused as to why I was so deep into the forest.

"I don't know. It's somewhere on the side of the mountain," I answered, really not sure where it was or how to find it.

"We'll help you. I'm a respiratory therapist, and this is my brother. When we get to where our vehicle is, we'll have to call the sheriff. Okay?" she asked very gently.

"Yes, that's okay," I replied. I had such an overwhelming feeling of relief that I was standing with two other people who I knew were going to help me.

They pulled out an emergency blanket from a large first aid kit and wrapped me in it. Then they gave me an all-weather jacket to keep warm for the ride out of the belly of the mountain.

I got on the back of the brother's ATV and held on to him around his waist. He was driving around forty miles an hour up the trail. My face was numb and freezing from the wind, but I was immersed in feeling like my life had been saved. Not completely in my right mind, but aware enough to know how lucky I was.

After the more than forty-five-minute ride, we arrived at the parking area for vehicles and trailers for ATVs. The super kind man led me to the front seat of his truck and turned on the heat full blast. The woman came over to me and handed me a bottle of orange Gatorade. I drank it quickly and then proceeded to projectile vomit all the liquid in my stomach.

For some reason, I trusted the woman knew what she was doing, but I was somewhat surprised when she told me I needed to take all my heavy, soaking wet clothes off. She said the wet clothes were contributing to hypothermia. I stripped down naked in front of two strangers, and they put the emergency blanket back on me. I was shivering so bad I was shaking. The multiple blisters on my thighs had turned into deep, oozing wounds, though I couldn't feel the pain because they were numb from the cold. The little toe on my right foot was blackened with frostbite.

I don't remember how long we waited for the sheriff and the ambulance to arrive. But eventually they came and drove me to a hospital in Coeur d'Alene, Idaho. The trip in the ambulance was much more pleasant than the ride to the hospital had been in Michigan. They started an IV fluid to treat my dehydration. Though they seemed to know I was struggling with my mental health, and they never restrained me, as that was not necessary. I may have been somewhat confused, but I wasn't a danger to anyone else.

After two nights in the hospital, they transferred me to the psych unit where I spent the next three weeks getting stabilized and having my wounds treated. The wounds on my legs were so bad they sent a wound care doctor to treat me. It took the entire time I was in the hospital for them to heal. The worst part was removing the bandages to take a shower. The burning sensation was so bad I cried from the pain.

They gave me an injection for a blood thinner that helped heal the frostbitten toes. Luckily, I didn't need to have my toe amputated. I just lost a few layers of flesh, and it left a sizeable scar, the remnants of a close call with the Grim Reaper.

~

Dr. Campbell, the psychiatrist who treated me in the hospital, walked into my room one day in the first week I was in the hospital. She said, "I've spoken to your family, and they're very worried about you. Why didn't you tell them where you were going?"

"My family is trying to poison me," I answered, pleading with her to believe me.

"Amy, you have to challenge your delusions. No one is trying to hurt you. This is a false belief," she stated gently yet directly.

"But look what they did to my head!" Still five years before learning the truth about my birthmark, I leaned forward and separated the hair from the bald spot on my head where the controversial birth mark existed. It was four years since Kendra had first made her comment about the birthmark. "My family pulled my hair out at birth, and now they're trying to poison me."

"How do you know they did this?" she asked.

"My therapist told me," I quickly answered while I glanced up at her as she stood over me.

"How would your therapist know what happened to you at birth? Does she have proof?" Finally, a mental health professional who I could trust had my best interest at heart and challenged Kendra. Immediately, when she questioned the validity of what Kendra had said to me, I realized in the moment my mind had been poisoned with false information. Almost like I was brainwashed in a weird kind of way. It was like I woke up from a bad dream and had a wave of relief I wasn't hurt by my family.

"Your family seems to care a lot about you. In my experience, people who show that much concern don't do things like that to hurt you. Your sister told me everyone has been very supportive of you. Is that true?" Dr. Campbell continued to talk with me in an exchange that was very reassuring. She reasoned with me and appealed to the part of me that was showing glimpses of being able to discern the difference between reality and false thoughts.

"Yes," I answered. "They've been supportive. But did they tell you what my cousin Joe did to me?" I asked very curiously.

"Yes, they told me about those incidents. But we're not going to focus on those things. You need to focus on getting well. Don't allow yourself to think about the past." Dr. Campbell spoke in a direct way and yet was not offensive. I found her to be understanding of my situation.

My stay in the Idaho psych unit was mostly pleasant. In all the inpatient hospitalizations I had, they were the most competent, kind, and caring people I had ever encountered. There was a nurse named Shirley, who used an old projector with slides and gave a small group of us a presentation about bipolar disorder. The most impactful statement Shirley made was, "You have bipolar disorder. It's a brain disorder, and it's not your fault!" Up until that point, over a thirteen-year time period, in my prior encounters with mental health care professionals, no one had ever explained to me the ins and outs of bipolar disorder. No one had ever told me I wasn't to be blamed for having an illness that was inherited. Her explanations and psychoeducation gave me a fighting chance to learn how to manage such a severe and complex illness.

It may have helped that the late actress Patty Duke, who lived with bipolar disorder, had visited the psych unit. The staff spoke about her as being an incredible mental health advocate who was so brave to have shared her story so others could benefit from her wisdom and insights. I was treated with the kind of respect and dignity that I had never before been treated with at a psych unit. This competent care and treatment plan put me on a pathway to recovery that I could have only wished happened years earlier.

Though they didn't focus a lot on PTSD, they did focus on treating the symptoms with a proper combination of medications. Even the mental health technicians, who have less training than social workers and psychiatric nurses, sat and talked to me.

One day a technician came into the library area where I was sitting by myself. She said, "Amy, I hope you know no matter what happened, you have nothing to be ashamed about. You can completely recover and live a full life."

I said, "Thank you for telling me this. Sometimes I feel like I'm 'crazy.'"

"You're not 'crazy,'" she stated with emphasis. "I'd like to bring in a movie I think would inspire you. It's about a woman named Temple Grandin, she has autism and has become an internationally known behaviorist. She's used her experiences and challenges to inform her work. You can do something like this one day with your experiences. Would you like for me to bring the movie in?"

"Yes! That would be awesome!" This conversation gave me so much hope. The technician was reinforcing the message Shirley had given me that no matter what happened, I could still rebuild my life. I could use my experiences to inform my work.

The next day, the technician brought the movie in, and a group of us watched it. I was deeply touched by Temple Grandin's story. I could feel my heart opening as I allowed myself to be inspired by someone else's journey. These inspiring lessons from Temple Grandin of never giving up would help me as I moved forward on my recovery journey.

Chapter 15

While in the hospital, I had the realization of how close I came to losing my life. The gravity of being lost in the forest was sinking in and creating a legitimate concern in my mind for my safety and well-being. I knew how critically important it was for me to stay mentally healthy, and at all costs do everything I could to keep myself from ever having another psychotic episode again.

In December 2012, I spent my forty-eighth birthday in the psych unit. They decided I was stable enough to be released a few days before New Year's Eve. I decided I was going to stay in Idaho for a while and go to the intensive outpatient treatment program the hospital psych unit provided. I felt as if I'd finally found professionals within the mental health treatment system who knew what they were doing and how to treat me. They gave me a folder with a number of resource phone numbers and potential places for lodging. One of the criteria for being released was having housing.

Prior to this point, I didn't know of any other options for finding competent mental health care professionals. It had begun to sink in how incompetent Dr. Richard and Kendra were. I was immensely saddened and disappointed to know the care I'd been receiving for over five years was way off the mark. I had so many examples of what could be considered malpractice in today's standard. In over five years of outpatient mental health treatment, I could have at the very least expected a proper diagnosis for the symptoms I was experiencing. The diagnosis was important because it tends to dictate a treatment plan. Although I had a history of bipolar disorder, they were only focusing on treating the symptoms of PTSD. The bipolar disorder was largely left untreated.

I made several phone calls to find a place to stay. There was a quaint place a few blocks from the hospital that primarily served cancer patients' families. I explained my situation to the manager of the care center, and she agreed to allow me to stay until I could make other housing arrangements.

The hospital security guard gave me a ride in the van to the care center. The two women who worked there, Mary and Beth, greeted me.

Mary was a hugger, and she didn't hesitate to give me a big hug when I arrived. After I settled into my room, I sat at the kitchen table with the women and talked about my experience in the wilderness.

"You said on the phone you're from West Virginia. How did you end up in Idaho?" Mary asked.

"Well, as I mentioned on the phone, I have bipolar disorder and PTSD. I got sick and ended up getting lost in the forest." As I said those words, it kind of sank into my soul on a deeper level just how fortunate I had been to have had my life saved.

"Wow! That must have been scary. But you're doing better now, right?" Beth chimed in and leaned forward in her chair.

"I had good mental health treatment in the hospital. So, I'm on the road to recovery. I hope I can help someone else one day, so they don't end up in my situation," I said as I glanced out the large window and daydreamed for a moment.

"Well, my family has dealt with mental illness. My grandson has several mental illnesses. He's having a really hard time," Beth said as her eyes teared up in an emotional moment.

"I'm sorry he's struggling. Don't give up hope. I believe recovery is possible for almost everyone," I said, kind of surprising myself with how much passion I conveyed.

For the next few days, Mary, Beth, and I would sit at the table and share a variety of stories. They were such lovely ladies. I was lucky to have crossed paths with them.

While I was in the hospital, I had been talking to my mother. She knew my intentions to stay in Idaho for a time where I could continue to receive mental health treatment. I don't know if she agreed with me or not, but she was supportive of what I wanted to do.

It was the end of December 2012, and I realized I left my travel portfolio with my driver's license on the side of a mountain in the forest. My mother had mailed me my checkbook so I could have access to my money, but with the exception of a local pharmacy, I couldn't cash a check without a driver's license. She also sent me a copy of my birth certificate so I could prove my identity. I decided to go to the DMV to get a driver's license. One of the women at the care center offered to give me a ride, but I opted to walk instead. My legs had finally healed, and the fresh air blowing on my cheeks was a small pleasure and a welcome benefit of being out of the hospital. I was also in awe of the beautiful mountains surrounding the town, and walking gave me the chance to enjoy nature's calming effects.

After a couple hours of walking, I finally arrived at the DMV. I gave the attendant all of my paperwork, and she told me to sit at the table equipped with a computer and take the written driver's test. She furrowed her brow and squinted while fidgeting in her chair. At the time, I thought she was behaving strangely because my circumstances were so out of the ordinary. I didn't know it at the time, but she was looking at me strangely because there was a warrant from Montana for my arrest. I later found this out when I was booked into jail.

It turns out the extra dog tag I had for Buddy the beagle that fell out of my Avalanche onto the ground had my name and phone number on it. This is how the sheriff in Montana figured out it was me who entered the log cabin and created a bit of a mess in the backyard.

After taking the driver's test, I walked back up to the counter and was immediately grabbed forcefully by the arm by a sheriff's deputy. He said, "Walk outside with me."

I followed his commands and walked outside while he put my arms behind my back and handcuffed me.

He said, "You know what you did." I said nothing in response as I had a full recollection of entering the home in Montana and knew it was wrong. The difference between this situation and what happened in Arizona was that I wasn't psychotic. I knew I needed to follow the directions of the sheriff. That was the difference for me between being in my right mind and not. I could easily comply with commands.

We arrived at the large county jail in Coeur d'Alene. It was December 30, and the inside of the jail was absolutely freezing cold. I was given a tan jumpsuit to put on and taken to a temporary cell block. While I waited for the intake, I made a phone call to my mother.

"You've got to help me," I rapidly said because I had a limited amount of time to talk.

"What's going on, Amy? Where are you?" my mother asked, sounding panicked.

"I'm in jail in Idaho. You've got to get me out of here!" I was so desperate, overwhelmed, and scared. I didn't know what my future held, but I knew I needed help.

"What did you do?" my mother asked sternly.

"I don't want to talk about it right now," I said, being very cautious about what I said on the phone. I guess I'd watched a few television programs and knew the phones in jail are recorded and monitored.

"Well, we'll get you out of there. Let me call Shelley, and we'll help you," she said, upbeat. Always the eternal optimist.

I hung up the phone and went back to the tiny holding cell.

After two days in the temporary holding cell, they moved me to the main population cell block. There were about twenty-five women housed in one cell block.

The jail staff were good about giving me my medications, as my mother had spoken to the sheriff and told him I needed my medication. My mother had called the director of the care center and asked her to bring my medications to the jail. Even though I'd only met her once, she did bring my medications for me. It was a real blessing to have people who were willing to help. I was also very blessed to have an advocate in my mother, who was always looking out for me. Since I was finally on the right combination of medication, it was easy to appreciate how blessed I was to have my mom's love and support.

I talked to many of the women and found out most had either a mental illness or substance use disorder. I was fascinated by their stories. Many of them had unfortunate circumstances and could have easily been the neighbor next door.

Sheila, one of the women I befriended, was quite familiar with the way jails and prisons functioned. She was clearly a frequent flyer, and she was very helpful in sharing information with me. Shelia said, "You're going to have to be extradited back to Montana. Don't worry about the small-town jail. It will look kind of creepy, but they'll probably be very friendly people. Don't let your imagination run wild." I listened intently to every word she said.

After around five days in the jail in Idaho, I was transferred to a small-town jail in Montana. When we arrived, I was fingerprinted and a mugshot was taken of me. All I did was passively follow all directions and stay extremely calm during the entire process. It's hard to describe how I felt emotionally. I wasn't disconnected from my emotions, but I was definitely more in my left brain mode, focused on what I needed to do to survive.

The cell block in the jail was extraordinarily little, especially compared to the jail in Idaho. There was a small television room with a metal table and four chairs, a shower, and then two separate jail cells with one set of metal bunks with a foam plastic mattress. There was a metal toilet with a small sink attached. The common area had the entrance to the jail cell and a small door with a sliding feed tray slot. There was a payphone in the cell block that I used frequently to call my mother. The jail cell was about enough to take four steps from the bunk to where the cell door was locked at night. It was large enough to allow me to only pace in a circle. There was one other inmate in the cell block with me, and her name was Terry.

After my first night in the jail, I had my arraignment hearing where they read the charges against me and asked me if I understood. I answered in the affirmative, as I had a copy of the charging documents. If I was convicted and given the maximum sentence on all charges, I was looking at twenty-plus years in prison. Turns out making a fire in someone's backyard was considered arson.

The first night in the jail cell was all so surreal. I was serious and sober, letting the charges against me sink into my bones. I knew I was potentially in a heap of trouble, but I refused to let myself think about the dread. I had to turn my attention to survival and acceptance. I thought to myself, *"It is what it is. I am where*

I am. I'm going to have to make the most of it."

The second morning, one of the corrections officers wheeled a portable library of magazines and books into the cell. I walked over to the cart, and one of the magazines I picked up had a front cover picture of my ex-partner Alexis's friend. She was not really my friend, though I'd been out to dinner with her, and she'd visited Alexis' and my home in Arizona on multiple occasions. She and Alexis had an emotionally intimate relationship the entire ten years Alexis and I were together, so naturally, I had a few emotions pop up when I saw her picture. How could I be so lucky to see a person I knew on the front cover of a magazine all the way in a jail cell in the mountains of Montana?

I picked up the magazine off the cart and took the four steps back toward my bunk. I sat down and started to read her recovery journey from cancer. Since there's not a lot to do in jail except read, write, and think, I had plenty of time to reflect on my failed ten-year relationship. I went through a gamut of emotions. One moment feeling guilty for ever leaving the relationship, and the next regretting ever having the relationship in the first place. There had simply been so many things happen to me since 2004 when the relationship ended that I never really had time or energy to reflect on it. In jail, time is about the only thing of real value. It was a time for me to re-examine my life.

In the cell, they allowed me to bring my folder with papers in it from the hospital. I also had a little blue Bible the hospital had given me. Terry gave me a pencil to write with. I began to use the pencil and paper and constructed a December and January calendar tracing my journey. I also kept a journal while in jail, recording my thoughts, feelings, and in general what I was doing to cope.

After a few days in jail, I met Greg, my public defender. I was let out of my cell to speak with him through a plastic partition and a phone. Greg's father-in-law had bipolar disorder, so he was well versed in understanding mental illness and specifically psychosis. Greg told me, "Anytime my father-in-law has an episode, he ends up in Las Vegas thinking he's a part of the mafia." I nodded in complete understanding.

From the very beginning, Greg was adamant that I was not guilty of any charges. He coached me to be patient and cooperate with the psychologist who would do an extensive examination of me. I suggested my family should post bail for me, but Greg convinced me the safest place for me was in the jail cell until I could go to my first appearance in court. I would have had to stay in the small town, and there really was nothing for me to do. Greg also wanted to make sure I was taking my medications. He knew the jail staff made sure I received the medications I needed. An interruption of a medication schedule could potentially have caused me to have a setback. Greg was really looking out for my best interest.

I passed the time in jail doing one of my favorite pastimes— reading. Of course, I read the magazine, and then I turned to fictional stories to stimulate my imagination and take my mind off of worrying about my fate. I also watched women's college basketball on television. I knew a few of the coaches I saw on television who had recruited me when I was in high school. There was always a moment of reflection, where I asked myself, "How did my life take such a downturn?" The only answer and solution I could come up with was convincing myself to focus on the things I could control and let go of the things I couldn't. I began practicing how to give myself a break and not judge myself so harshly for struggling with my mental health. At the time, I did do a fair amount of blaming myself for landing in jail. I asked myself, "How could I have let this happen to me?"

When I look back, I'd say the most intriguing thing I did was allow myself to dream. I decided in that jail cell to try to use everything I had learned to help other people. Even in the early parts of my recovery journey, I had helped and coached young people with a positive, encouraging style. I'd managed to train co-workers using the knowledge and expertise I accumulated.

I wanted to become a peer coach, a mental health advocate, and speaker, and I wanted to write books. I could have just as easily given up and felt sorry for myself. But giving up wasn't my nature. I had a sheer determination from my inner voice that no matter what happened I was not going to let the negative forces in my life defeat me. I perceived those negative forces were Dr. Richard, Kendra, Belinda, and the four perpetrators from my past who had directly caused my mental health to deteriorate. In my mind, it was another battle of what I perceived as the evil and the good. Again, I convinced myself the good was going to win. I took a page out of my mother's book that said, "Everything is going to work out." I really believe my attitude helped shape my experience from what could have been absolutely horrible, into using the time to create a vision of things I could do to help myself and others.

In January 2013, after about two weeks in jail, I asked one of the corrections officers if I could be a helper. As a helper, I prepared meals in the kitchen for other inmates, washed laundry, and mopped floors. In return, I'd be let out of the cell block and have a bit of freedom. It was my way of passing the time and making the best out of the situation.

Prior to becoming a jail helper, the day finally came for me to have my first appearance in court. As if I needed to be more humbled, I learned what it was like to have handcuffs on and my ankles shackled. Getting to court from my cell was a two-step shuffle. In a first appearance, the charges against me were read and I entered my plea of "not guilty" to all the charges. If anything could be positive from this, the entire experience provided motivation for me to do everything I could to help prevent someone else with mental illness from having to ever go through an intersection with the criminal justice system.

I was adamant at the time that my experience was not going to be wasted on self-pity and helplessness. I sort of had this internal knowing what I was living through wasn't by any means pleasant, but there was tremendous wisdom and value I could mine from the experience.

A few days after the first appearance, the prosecutor agreed to allow me to be released to the custody of my sister, Shelley. She had to fly to Montana and escort me back to West Virginia with a GPS ankle bracelet attached.

I sat waiting outside the probation officer's office for Shelley to arrive. I stared out the window and could see the snow hanging on the evergreen trees. I pondered the thought of freedom. The warmth and contentment of feeling as if my life and my freedom really mattered. Something I would never again take for granted. After many years of numbing my emotions during difficult situations, I was filled with an overwhelming feeling of gratitude. I was still worried about what my future might hold, but I was hopeful in the moment things would get better.

Shelley arrived and greeted me with a smile and a loud, "Hi, Amy. Let's go get something to eat."

I laughed and kind of enjoyed the fact she didn't treat me any differently. Her task oriented "let's do this" attitude was contagious. My head still had some worrying thoughts, but my heart was filled with the fact I had a sister who loved me enough to travel all the way across the country to get me out of jail and take me back home to West Virginia.

Chapter 16

It was the beginning of February 2013, my first night at home. I left the light on in my room and closed my eyes to go to sleep. I could see the image of my jail cell. I opened my eyes and noticed an oil painting I had purchased when I lived in Payson, Arizona. It was a beautiful picture of a lake, an eagle perched on a tall tree, and a snow-capped mountain in the background. It reminded me of the backpacking trip I took in Montana many years prior to becoming an inmate. In that painting was a reminder of all the beautiful things I saw and experienced. I took a deep breath and focused on how much joy I had. I told myself *nothing bad is happening right now.* Some of the strategies I had learned from Dr. Campbell and the staff in Idaho were very beneficial. I made a mental note to balance my memories and focus on not only the unpleasant part of my experiences, but on the positive as well. This shift in thinking provided an overwhelming relief for my mental health. It was the first step in putting everything in perspective, and though it would take several years to get to a place of reconciled peace, I would, in fact, eventually get there.

Within the first week of returning to West Virginia, I was set up with an appointment with my mom's psychiatrist of many years, Dr. Andronic. I had met Dr. Andronic when I accompanied my mother on a few of her appointments. I'm not sure why I didn't see Dr. Andronic years earlier. It seems obvious now that I could have benefited from being under her care. She didn't specialize in trauma, but she was an expert in treating and understanding symptoms. I learned a diagnosis is important to a degree, but more important is being able to articulate symptoms. Diagnostic criteria are often on a continuum, which is why two people with similar symptoms can be diagnosed with two different illnesses. It often depends on who the psychiatrist is and how they interpret someone's symptoms.

Dr. Andronic didn't focus so much on fitting me into a specific label. She turned her attention on the specifics she knew would keep me mentally healthy. At every visit, the first question she asked was, "How much are you sleeping?" I came to learn sleeping too much or too little is often an indicator of a mental health state. In my case, a significant reduction in sleep often triggered a manic episode. For me, lack of sleep for multiple days in a row was an indication I was getting sick. Learning such a simple strategy helped me to stay mentally healthy.

My initial visit with Dr. Andronic was incredibly refreshing. She listened to my story with compassion and understanding. Dr. Andronic treated me with an incredible amount of dignity and respect. In my first visit, she said, "What happened to you wasn't your fault. You have so much potential and talent. You're going to recover. Just work with me, and you'll get better every day." This initial visit set the tone for a healthy, therapeutic relationship that would last nearly eight years.

In addition to seeing Dr. Andronic, I began seeing a new therapist, Jane. She was in the same office as Dr. Andronic. Initially, my visits with both of my new mental health professionals were very frequent. Dr. Andronic saw me every two weeks for a few months, and I saw Jane every week for several months.

In my first visit with Jane, she said, "Amy, you're thinking of yourself as a little kid sitting at the table with pizza all over your mouth. We see you as a strong woman who is talented and smart. I hope you can start seeing yourself the same way. See yourself as more than your illness." Her honest, insightful feedback was always welcomed in our sessions. In contrast to Kendra, Jane listened without judgment. She came to know me well enough to realize I didn't need someone to point out my shortcomings, as I did that really well myself. I needed someone to remind me of all the good I had to offer.

Sometimes it didn't take much for me to have a shift in my

thinking. This is why having a psychiatrist and therapist who encouraged me to focus on my strengths was so beneficial. I think it was somewhat of an automatic response to ruminate over all the things I could have done better regarding my mental health conditions. But both Dr. Andronic and Jane encouraged me to reset my thinking, learn from what I could have done better, and focus on moving forward with my life.

Looking back, I'd say it was an intense commitment to mental health treatment that I could have benefited from years earlier. Sometimes getting on the right track with mental health treatment takes some kind of tragic outcome. It's unfortunate, but true in many cases.

While at home in West Virginia, I wore the GPS monitor for a few weeks, and by April 2013, my case had finally worked its way through the system. I'm not going to lie and say it was easy waiting for a decision by the court. It was a slow grind, every single day. I focused as much as humanly possible in the present, savoring the taste of a good cup of coffee and focusing on all the little things that made big differences. Despite my realization that Dr. Richard and Kendra could have provided better care, there were some things I learned that I found helpful. The constant reminder of staying in the present moment was one of those tips.

There was significant stress of knowing my fate hung in the balance. The major differences between the Montana incident and what happened in Arizona was the fact I was stabilized on the proper medications, I wasn't isolated, and I had an extremely great attorney who put me at ease anytime I spoke to him.

Eventually, the prosecutor agreed to drop all the charges against me, as long as I followed through with three years of treatment. Dr. Andronic would write letters every three months for three years, and I would send them to the prosecutor's office to demonstrate I was actually following through with a treatment plan. It turns out the one benefit of having seen Dr. Richard for nearly five years was I had a significant amount of documentation in my healthcare records. The psychologist who did the evaluation for the court had done an exceptional job of obtaining all the information that proved I was, in fact, not a criminal, but a person who was a victim of poor mental health treatment and a documented history of having serious mental illness with a significant trauma history from childhood sexual abuse.

Greg saved me from potentially dire consequences. And the court believed my story. This acknowledgement was a validation for me that without a shadow of a doubt what happened to me was not my fault, even though I'd have to work on not blaming myself for what happened.

By the summer of 2013, the court issues were resolved for the most part, my internal and external wounds from being lost in the wilderness were healed, and I was actively figuring out a way to move forward with my life.

I decided part of my recovery was getting a job and returning to work. I had to take small steps to rebuild my confidence, all the while processing the consequences of my psychotic episode. I was making big strides in recovery, in part because I had so much support. In addition to having quality mental health professionals, I also continued to benefit from family support. My mother and Shelley had always been there for me. My nieces Natalie and Ashley, and my great nephew, Tony, all showered me with the kind of unconditional love that filled up my heart. No one in my family blamed me or judged me for what happened, and they all believed I could recover. Almost every step on my recovery journey, I had someone along the way cheering for me.

Tony and I would take walks through the woods and spend time playing video games. These lighthearted activities gave me a break from thinking about the seriousness of my past circumstances and helped me to heal.

During the summer in 2013, in a full circle moment, my family and I took a vacation to Cape Hatteras, North Carolina—the same place I'd taken an RV trip back in 2008. These new experiences began my replacement of struggle and strife to having many pleasant experiences and making new memories. I was really struggling with grief, though. The grief of losing a life I had worked hard to build, the dreams that were no longer obtainable, and coming to terms with the effects of an undertreated mental illness. The grieving process allowed me to honor my pain, release the hurt, and live more fully in the present.

In September 2013, I began working a retail job for $7.25 an hour, minimum wage. Although I had to withdraw from the PhD program, I had a master's degree and almost eighteen years working in corporate America at a manager level. I knew I was underemployed based on my resume. The on-paper version of "Amy" was very different than the battered, full life version of her. But I didn't care how much money I made; I knew I needed to interact with people. Talking to people and telling someone to "have nice day" made me feel good. The more I worked, the more my head cleared. I was well on my way to recovering.

In the next two years, my focus was on living my life. I took multiple trips with my family, attended a wedding, went to the gym, spent time outside, and played with my nephew. It took some time to find the right combination of medications, but for the most part I didn't focus on the past. I learned many self-help strategies by reading articles of people who lived with mental illness on the Internet. I read books about bipolar disorder and PTSD. This allowed me to come to terms with how my life had been so drastically upended. I knew I wasn't alone, and that gave me a sense of belonging. I came to realize I wasn't "odd," "crazy," or "nuts." I was just a person who needed the proper mental health treatment to find wellness.

In retrospect, I believe the mental health treatment I received from Dr. Andronic was one of the key factors for moving my focus on living my life. Our conversations were always about recovery. She never once asked me to recall any of the traumatic events that had caused me so much suffering. Dr. Andronic was much more focused on how my symptoms and experiences were affecting me in the "now," not the past. She consistently encouraged me to believe I was an intelligent and talented woman who happened to have my life interrupted by mental illness.

Dr. Andronic consistently told me I was much more than my diagnosis. Even though I had encountered multiple psychiatrists who gave me many reasons not to trust anyone had my best interest at heart, I wholeheartedly trusted and believed Dr. Andronic. I embraced what she taught me and quickly came to believe I could get better and rebuild my life.

Chapter 17

While my part-time job didn't challenge me intellectually, it did provide structure and much needed interaction with other people. It was really important for me to feel "normal." In my conversations with Jane and Dr. Andronic, they continually reinforced the idea that if I kept working to recover and build my life, I would naturally heal in time.

When I wasn't working, I spent a great deal of time in my recovery journey researching what resources were available with mental health advocacy organizations in other parts of the country. I kept finding a gap in services offered in my local community, and I wanted to find a way to offer others impacted by mental illness support and resources. I continued to write articles on my blog, but I wanted to do more.

After a couple of years of working in retail, I had an opportunity to take all the knowledge I'd gathered and make good on my vision in jail of becoming a mental health advocate and speaker. I started writing a blog called "Shedding Light on Mental Health" in January 2014. I made a decision when I first pressed "publish" on the blog that I was going to publicly disclose my mental health diagnosis. It was a step I didn't take lightly, as I was well aware how much stigma existed when it came to mental illness. The stigma was one of the main reasons I decided to disclose my diagnosis. I hoped by speaking up and sharing my experience I might be able to help one other person. I might even be able to change one person's mind about how they perceived someone with mental illness.

In the summer of 2014, I attended a local chapter of National Alliance on Mental Illness meeting (NAMI). While introducing myself, I blurted, "My name is Amy Gamble. I live with bipolar disorder, and I want to be a mental health advocate." It was appropriate for that kind of meeting, though most everyone who was there were family members of loved ones who had mental illness. During that meeting, I met Libby, a NAMI Greater Wheeling board member who asked me to speak at their upcoming Candlelight Vigil Service in September. Each year, the local chapter held the event, and it was often covered by the media.

I was so nervous walking into the large church where my first in-person public disclosure of mental illness was about to take place. I worried if people would perceive me differently if they knew some things about my history with mental illness. Public speaking was something I'd done off and on throughout my life, starting way back when I was in high school. I also developed speaking and presentation skills throughout my time in the pharmaceutical industry. And so, when I walked up to the front of the church and stood behind that microphone, it was a familiar feeling to be in front of an audience. Yet I can't say I was filled with a huge amount of confidence. Confidence building was an intentional endeavor and would take time to re-build.

I didn't give much thought to the possibility of being in the newspaper the next day, but that's what happened. Former Olympian and mental illness make for an interesting combination for a newspaper headline. Once I started sharing my journey with mental illness publicly, there was no such thing as going back in hiding, although there were a few occasions when I would question the reasons I was self-disclosing.

I was thrilled when Libby contacted me and asked me to become a member of the NAMI of Greater Wheeling board of directors. This opened the door for me to help bring support for others in the community.

In the summer of 2015, the board of directors agreed to allow me to become the Executive Director of NAMI of Greater Wheeling. I had left my retail job to take the position and devote my time and energy to mental health advocacy. I had a fairly big vision for the advocacy group. My research had given me many ideas for what other chapters were doing around the country, and I wanted to focus the organization on providing mental health information, education, support, and resources for the community. I used my platform as an athlete to help create brand awareness and increase exposure for the non-profit organization.

Many of the NAMI board members were supportive of my efforts, but my biggest champion and supporter was always Libby. Her encouragement and genuine support opened many doors for me. Our personal and professional relationship was one of the keys to my recovery journey. I'm eternally grateful to have had Libby in my life.

Shortly after I began leading the organization, I met Bill, a local philanthropist and well-known mentor in the recovery community. He was active in helping many local non-profit organizations by providing mentoring and guidance to many local leaders. Bill was also known for his artistic endeavors, often sketching people in the community. He was interesting and unique.

In our first lunch date, Bill said, "We don't need pomp and circumstance. To eliminate feeling awkward, do you mind if I read you a poem?"

I was immediately touched and responded, "Sure, that would be great!" He and I instantly became friends. He was in his late eighties and full of wisdom, compassion for his fellow human being, and had the energy of a man half his age. Bill didn't know a lot of my history with mental illness, but he knew enough to know I'd been through some tough times. On our second lunch date, he brought me a book and wrote me a note inside the front cover. The book was "No Mud No Lotus: The Art of Transforming Suffering" by Thich Nhat Hanh.

The concept that all of humanity suffers in some way or another was something that deeply struck my soul. On the pathway to healing was a long process of a deep level of acceptance for all of my experiences. The book taught me to let go of judgment of either good or bad and simply breathe deeply and accept whatever my experiences had been. It didn't mean I had to like something, forgive people, or forget what happened. I just had to learn to accept it.

When I reflected on all I'd experienced, I gave a lot of thought to the idea of forgiving my abusers. Forgive? For a very long time I didn't think I could forgive. I've since learned forgiveness is really powerful. It doesn't mean I condone, suppress my memories, or pretend that what happened wasn't horrific. Forgiveness is my conscious choice. Resentment festers and comes out in a variety of ways. Holding on to resentment only hurts me. I came to the understanding through my spiritual practices that I needed to let go. With that said, forgiveness has not been a simple act. It's been a process and will probably take me a lifetime. But every step I take closer to forgiveness allows me to move forward with a lighter heart and, most importantly, with inner peace.

The active practice of forgiveness has allowed me to uncover the grief I've carried for years. The heavy burden of being an innocent child who crossed paths with adults who probably carried their own wounds. Where I am with forgiveness allows me to have compassion for the kind of wounds my abusers must have carried to be capable of carrying out such a horrific act. Then again, I don't really know why adults hurt children. It probably would serve me well to stop asking why they did what they did.

I've never forgotten the sexual assaults. I probably have accepted more than I have forgiven at this point. I accept what happened to me as a fact, so I don't have to hold on to resentments, vengeance, and anger. I will never forget. I don't and never will excuse, condone, or minimize what they did to me. I suffered substantially and paid an enormous price to reclaim my mental health. I worked very hard to heal the painful wounds. Forgiveness sounds good and sometimes unintentionally sounds trite, but acceptance has been more important to me. Acceptance was like giving me an open window so the haunting ghosts of the past could be released.

As I worked on acceptance, I found myself imagining I was in a stream with rapids running with white caps. If I kept fighting the flow of the stream I was going to drown. The key to surviving in rapid waters was to let go and allow the stream to carry me until I was in peaceful waters. This was my analogy for coming to terms with my suffering and all that I had experienced that was traumatic, tragic, or unpleasant.

I would also talk about my personal discoveries with Bill.

Although he grew up in the Catholic Church, he and I would have these deep discussions on Buddhist teachings. We would often meet at a local golf club restaurant surrounded by beautiful trees and putting greens. Every time I'd see him, he would ask, "Amy, do you meditate? I think it would really help you. It's healing, you know?"

"Yes, Bill. I'm meditating. I'm using guided meditation. Some days it's easier than others," I answered with a smile. I had this great sense of satisfaction and in some ways relief that I finally had a friend who understood me and my deep nature.

A couple of the many things that were so beautiful about Bill was he was so incredibly encouraging and honest. He would say gently, "Amy, you have so much potential. But I don't think you have any confidence."

I'd respond in the affirmative. "You're right, Bill. I'm working on rebuilding my confidence." The thing about Bill's feedback was it never felt uncomfortable. He just had a way of being direct and honest without being hurtful.

Bill's understanding and compassion toward people with mental illness came from many of his family members who lived with mental illness. He'd seen their suffering firsthand and knew mental illness didn't discriminate.

Bill said, "It doesn't matter if you're rich or poor. Mental illness can affect anyone from all socioeconomic levels." This understanding and close to home effect drove Bill's desire to help me grow NAMI of Greater Wheeling into the big vision I had for the organization.

With Bill's and Libby's encouragement and the support of a local foundation, I went to work obtaining instructor certifications in Mental Health First Aid. Mental Health First Aid (MHFA) is an eight-hour educational course that teaches people how to respond to someone who is experiencing a mental health crisis.

One of my favorite parts of the MHFA class was teaching people about psychosis. In one of my classes full of schoolteachers, one gentleman was brave enough to say, "People who have psychosis are possessed by the devil!" It really makes me laugh now, but it's also a lingering reality of a portion of the population who really don't understand mental illness very well.

When he made that statement, I debated for a brief moment on what I was going to say. At one time his comment would have made me feel ashamed, but I had come so far in my recovery journey that I didn't feel shame. I felt more determined to make a difference and try to help people understand. I didn't always use self-disclosure to make a point, but in that case, I felt it was imperative to shed light on a very misunderstood topic.

I looked directly at the man who made the comment about psychosis, took a deep breath, and said, "I actually had a psychotic episode, and I wasn't demonically possessed." I certainly had a few chuckles in the class. I learned that day by reading the class evaluations that while all the statistics and information were important, it was my personal story that made the biggest impact. From that point on, I began to share brief personal vignettes during the discussion about psychosis.

At the same time, I began teaching classes. I started reaching out to local schools, colleges, and churches to schedule mental health talks and trainings. These efforts allowed me to tap into my skill set and naturally build confidence every step of the way.

Finally, after struggling for so many years with symptoms of mental illness, I had my conditions under control, the past in a somewhat neat box, and my mind was focused on making a difference in people's lives—one talk and training at a time.

Chapter 18

In the spring of 2016, my high school contacted me and asked me to give a commencement speech to the graduating class. I was honored by the request and looked forward to giving the speech. Instead of being held in the high school auditorium, the ceremony was held in a local arena. This was a relief to me that I didn't have to go stand in the auditorium where the past trauma had occurred. It was also somewhat of a monumental decision because I had generally avoided anything related to my high school. Many years later, I learned one of the stages in PTSD is avoidance. By making a decision to give that speech, I was actively taking steps in my recovery journey from PTSD.

By the time I gave the commencement address, I had plenty of experience in public speaking, as I had given over fifty talks and trainings to various audience sizes in the course of a year. There was actually something very magical about using my past experiences to reach audiences of all ages.

In the commencement speech I gave, the audience was well over two thousand people. The graduates were directly in front of the main stage. All the school administrators sat on the stage with me. As I walked up to the podium, I could feel an overwhelming amount of gratitude inside. While my leg was shaking behind the podium, my voice was strong and unwavering. I knew how fortunate I was to have opportunities, not to rewrite my past, but to write my present and future in a way that could bring me satisfaction and pleasure. I always found a great deal of self-satisfaction in helping other people.

As I looked into the bright eyes of the young people, I had the opportunity to acknowledge one of the kids I had trained in basketball. I looked into the audience and could see Shelia sitting there. I met eyes with her and said, "I want to take a minute to congratulate one of your classmates on breaking my thirty-plus year scoring record." I could see Shelia smiling as her classmates erupted into loud cheers. The audience applauded, whistled, and celebrated her achievement.

In the speech, I talked about the importance of having dreams. With every word I chose, I made a point of noting how sometimes in life not everyone is going to be supportive of our dreams. I said, "There will be times in life when we fail and come up short of our goals." I used my story of transferring from the University of Tennessee and how I initially felt like a failure. Four years later, I walked into the Olympic stadium. I told the graduates, "There's often not a straight line in striving for a dream. Sometimes others will be supportive, but what matters most is that we believe in ourselves and that we hold on to our dreams."

I wasn't coming from a place of a trite "dream big" mentality. I was speaking from experience in the self-actualization of having the great fortune of dreams coming true. I was a long way from the jail cell in Montana, where I wrote down on paper what I wanted to achieve. Even in that experience was a place where having dreams helped me cope with an unfortunate circumstance. I didn't share that hardship, but I had quite a few examples of coming up short in life. Up until that point, I had walked my journey in life with enough adversity to know wholeheartedly that sometimes believing in a dream can be the difference between giving up and tenaciously forging onward.

When the valedictorian came to the podium to give his speech, he said, "Didn't you enjoy Amy Gamble's speech? I really liked what she had to say." The crowd gave an approving applause. The acknowledgement that my words made a difference gave me great gratitude.

Also, in the audience that night was my own personal cheering section, Libby, my mother, and my sister, Shelley. They were so proud of me. It really touched my heart to know I had an infusion of support and encouragement. The people who mattered most to me and knew almost all of my history smiled the biggest and clapped the most. On the ride home, I felt a great deal of satisfaction and had a smile on my face. Most importantly, I had a feeling of peace knowing I was using my experiences to help other people.

The next day one of the headlines in the local newspaper was, "Olympian Tells Graduates to Follow Dreams." Seeing that article was the exclamation point on my message. Receiving external validation and making an impact was a gift I didn't take for granted. I knew at the time how fortunate I was to have had the background and experiences that allowed me to share my knowledge with others. Giving to others helped me in return to build confidence.

Dr. Andronic continued to be a key supporter of mine who reminded me frequently to remember all of who I was. She said, "Amy, you're fortunate to have had all these experiences you can build on. A lot of people have had their lives disrupted by mental illness when they were very young. You had the opportunity to accumulate lots of experiences. Remember those experiences. They'll help you recover." The continuous reminders that I was much more than my diagnoses helped me build on my strengths.

I naturally shifted from being hyper-focused on my past traumas to embracing all of my experiences. I learned it was critically important to see myself as a whole human being. Not a label. Not a "sick" person. Dr. Andronic encouraged me to see myself and my life in balance. As difficult and traumatic as coming to terms with being a victim was, it was in fact a snapshot in time. Certainly, a part of my history, but it wasn't all of who I was. I reminded myself that I am a survivor and have worked through my past pains. I needed to remember the gift of having been an Olympic athlete, because remembering those positive experiences and all the adversity I had to overcome to get there was a jolt my system needed.

Sometimes I would sit in Dr. Andronic's office and feel amazed at how she seemed to understand me so well. Although I had generally felt quite uncomfortable with my other psychiatrists, she had a way of putting me at ease. She made me feel like a human being and not a "sick" person. Having her as a psychiatrist changed my life in more ways than one. Dr. Andronic would spend forty-five minutes with me on every visit. It was supposed to be only fifteen minutes, but she never adhered to that practice. In those visits, she educated me about the importance of sleep for my mental health, the many symptoms I'd need to watch out for, and she worked with me to find the right combination of medications that didn't make me feel like a zombie. Having such a great psychiatrist allowed me to contrast my experiences with Dr. Richard. There was quite a difference between the two in so many ways. I felt fortunate I was finally under the treatment of someone who was exceptional.

~

By the end of 2017, I had given over a hundred mental health talks and trainings since I'd gotten started two years earlier. I was driven to teach what I had learned, in hopes it may help someone else. I had come to realize how incredibly healing it was for me to share my story in front of audiences. I wanted to provide that same opportunity for a group of people in the community.

As part of my research of what other people were doing around the country to raise awareness for mental illness, I came upon an organization who was putting on a literal show with people who had mental illness. I brought the idea to one of my colleagues and we decided to do a show at the Capitol Theatre in Wheeling, West Virginia. The show was called *This is My Brave*. The concept and This is My Brave organization were co-founded by a fellow mental health advocate and bipolar warrior, Jennifer Marshall. Jennifer's fearless and bold attitude fueled the movement for people with mental illness to share their stories on stage. Her organization helped event organizers all over the world emulate her vision that "storytelling saves lives."

The Wheeling show had sixteen local people who lived with mental illness or a substance use disorder—or both—share their experiences on the stage through either music lyrics, spoken word, poetry, or a brief story. Though a third of the theatre was filled, it was a nice sized crowd from the community that came out to support the event. Two television crews came out to cover the story. On that night, we took a huge, bright light and quite literally shined it on the faces of those who lived with mental illness. It was a night to remember. I was touched by the joy, happiness, and empowerment the participants experienced.

While doing the talks, trainings, and events took up a great deal of my time and energy, I was also involved as part of a steering committee with the local police chief for a Crisis Intervention Training (CIT) program he was trying to get started for his staff and potentially others around the state of West Virginia. NAMI of Greater Wheeling had been asked to have representation on the committee. I actually had gone to the same high school as the police chief, and he showed a great deal of respect for me as a former athlete and a human being.

The first time in years that I had seen the police chief, he was speaking at a mental health conference NAMI Greater Wheeling had hosted at a local venue with about a hundred people in attendance. The chief was on a panel with several community leaders discussing what their organizations were doing to support people living with mental illness.

I walked up to him after his talk and shared with him what happened to me in Arizona with the police. I was convinced that if the police in Arizona had CIT, they would have handled the situation with me in a more delicate manner. I wouldn't have been treated like a criminal and traumatized unnecessarily. I would have been treated like someone who needed medical attention, in the same way a person who had a physical illness would be treated.

After hearing my story, the chief said to me, "I'm so sorry that happened to you. That's why we want to implement the training here, to prevent those things from occurring."

I nodded and said, "Thank you for listening to my story. It really helps me to talk about it."

A couple of years after I first spoke to the police chief, I attended the first CIT committee meeting. I was a little overwhelmed with a flood of memories from my Arizona experience. The meeting was held in a conference room at a local news station. There were fifteen people in attendance who were considered stakeholders. Two other people from NAMI of Greater Wheeling were with me. I kept pinching myself at the thought of being in the same room with the police chief and working on a project together. I thought, "What was the likelihood I'd ever find myself in this position?" For a long time after my

Arizona experience with law enforcement, I would cringe when I'd see a police car, flashing lights, or a police officer.

As I did with many other things that were traumatic, I immersed myself in situations where I confronted my fears. I found my way through these situations on my own, never really addressing any of it in therapy. Instead, I turned to books and articles I'd found on the Internet and implemented what I had learned. It was never easy to do these things, but in the end, it was totally worth it.

As part of my commitment to promoting the CIT program, I went to the local police department and talked to the officers at the beginning of their shifts. The first time I walked in the doors of the police station, I had this surreal feeling, shaking my head in disbelief. On one hand, feeling empowered. On the other hand, feeling completely vulnerable. I blocked out the uncomfortable feelings of tingling nerves and found myself in a large conference room standing in front of police officers and teaching them about psychosis. This was not a speaking event I looked forward to. It was something I had to mentally prepare for. It's a blur to me how many officers were in the room. While the experience was unnerving, in comparison to being lost in the wilderness, it wasn't really that scary.

In 2018, I filmed a commercial for a local non-profit organization focusing on First Episode Psychosis. The youth organization offered behavioral health services to youth up to the age of eighteen. The organization wanted to use my name and sports background to draw attention and raise awareness that there is help for someone who experiences psychosis. The message was the importance of early intervention, just like any other disease. The connection with the CIT program was the fact that law enforcement officers often encounter people who experience a mental health crisis. One such crisis is when a person is experiencing psychosis.

I don't know if I realized it at the time, but I was putting a name and a face on psychosis. Psychotic episodes are far more common than people realize. Episodes occur in three out of one hundred people. During a psychotic episode, it often puts a person experiencing it in contact with the police. Not in every case, but in many.

~

By the summer of 2019, I was selected by a local non-profit organization to attend the CIT International Conference in Seattle, Washington. I was asked to receive training as a CIT coordinator and bring back the key learnings so I could share with other people on the CIT committee. In this role, I would help coordinate CIT training for law enforcement officers. I found myself in a unique position where all my past experiences and perspective were seen as a tremendous value by others. I had insights only someone with mental illness who interacted with the police could have, and at that point I had over four years of experience in being a fierce mental health advocate.

When I arrived at the hotel in downtown Seattle, the entire lobby was swarming with law enforcement officers, many in blue uniforms. It was a little bit intimidating. I'll be honest; I did question why I agreed to put myself in that position. I could feel a general sense of uneasiness and a churning stomach caused by nervous anxiety. I handled the situation by quickly checking into my room. I took a deep breath and talked myself through the anxiety I was feeling. I used a lot of positive affirmations and was very gentle with my self-talk. I had to mentally prepare myself for being in a training the next day with over a hundred police officers. I stood looking out the window with a view of the famous Seattle Space Needle. In a moment of distraction from the stress I was feeling, even though I don't like heights, I decided I was going to walk to the Space Needle and take the elevator up to the six hundred feet overlook. I think I was focused on facing my fears in more ways than one.

One of the nice things about my experience in working in the pharmaceutical industry was I was very accustomed to attending conferences and meetings with lots of people. In some ways, working my way down the escalator the next morning and into the large ballroom was like riding a bike for me. Something that was natural and familiar. It was similar and yet so different.

The good news was most of the law enforcement officers in attendance were there voluntarily, which meant they chose to receive the training on how to help someone experiencing a mental health crisis. They were as motivated as I was to learn new information. The entire experience reset my feelings toward law enforcement. It gave me a renewed sense of hope that there were actually people who cared about helping someone experiencing a mental health crisis. I had firsthand experience in how a situation was handled poorly. I was realistic in knowing the training may not eliminate all negative outcomes, but I was certain it could provide some people to have help and not handcuffs.

On the first day of the conference, I ran into Becky, an old friend I knew from my days living at the Olympic Training Center. Becky had become a police officer in Tempe, Arizona. Somehow, she picked me out of the crowd and came up to say hello.

"Hi. I'm Becky, originally from Colorado. Aren't you Amy Gamble, the team handball player?" she asked with a big smile on her face.

"Yes! I'm Amy Gamble." This time when I said my name, I said it with confidence and not with desperation, indicating where I was on my life journey.

"I remember watching you at the Olympic Training Center. Are you a police officer? What are you doing here?" she asked, noticing I wasn't in a blue uniform.

"No, I'm not a cop," I said, kind of chuckling. "I'm with a local chapter of NAMI, and I'm here to learn about CIT, so I can take what I learn back to my community," I answered without much wavering in my voice, although I was quite shocked to run into someone I knew from my past. Then again, it seemed to be more like the rule and not the exception for me to have uncanny encounters with people.

"Let's sit together during the general session and catch up," Becky said and gave me a big hug.

I walked away from that encounter and kind of shook my head. Crossing paths with people I knew at different times in my life was somewhat surprising, but really more of a representation of how eclectic my life experiences had been.

The next day during the conference, I saw Becky and a fellow police officer who was her partner. During lunch time, we sat at a large, round conference table talking.

"How did you get interested in CIT?" Becky asked, not knowing what kind of answer I was going to give her.

I took a deep breath and decided to share my Arizona experience with the two of them. "I had an encounter with police officers in Arizona during a psychotic episode," I said in response.

"Oh, really?" Becky asked, clearly surprised by my answer.

"Yes, it was really unpleasant and affected me for a very long time. I decided to use my experience to provide some insights to police officers through CIT." I went on to explain what happened on that sweltering hot day in the Arizona desert way back in 2006.

Becky and her partner sat listening with genuine interest. Their smiles in the beginning of our conversation turned to a sober look. I could see in their eyes they were sad for me. They seemed somewhat intrigued by the whole story. I had a liberating feeling. A sense of freedom and empowerment that came from sharing my vulnerabilities and subsequent fears. Their supportive listening and compassion confirmed my inner knowledge that there was truly healing in revealing. I felt touched by the fact I could use my story to provide perspective to two people who truly cared about helping someone experiencing a mental health crisis.

In retrospect, I realize how fortunate and blessed I was to have had the opportunity to take my challenging experiences and use the wisdom and knowledge gained in a way that might help someone else. When I was walking down my life path, I wasn't thinking about the impact I was making. My focus was on making a difference with my mental health advocacy efforts one person at a time.

Chapter 19

In November 2019, I had the opportunity to attend an Olympic and Paralympic Alumni reunion in Colorado Springs, Colorado. There were so many things going through my mind when I stepped foot back onto the grounds of the Olympic Training Center. I hadn't seen most of my teammates for years, yet I'd followed many of them on Facebook. Several people knew of my work as a Mental Health Advocate and were aware I had bipolar disorder. I spoke to a few people about incorporating Mental Health First Aid training for national team coaches.

After becoming aware of my mental health advocacy work, the US Olympic and Paralympic personnel who work on the annual Team USA calendar contacted me in 2020 and said they wanted to use my name and image in the 2022 calendar. They selected me for the month of May, which is Mental Health Awareness month. Considering my path to becoming a mental health advocate, being selected for the Team USA calendar was a wonderful feeling. It was like I had climbed a huge mountain and was now standing at the top looking down at where I had come from. The exhilarating feeling of being recognized for using my platform to help other people added another layer to my healing. I never needed much external validation, but it was nice to know my work was having an impact.

At this time in my life, I had confidence enough to put myself back in positions where I was living my life beyond my diagnosis. Dr. Andronic had spent seven years reassuring me I could recover and encouraged me to focus on my strengths, which boosted my self-confidence. I had invested hundreds of hours teaching people about mental health conditions and the importance of seeking help and learning how to help others.

The added benefit of being open about my diagnosis often opened the door for other people to have someone they could go to who would understand even the most complicated situations resulting from mental illness. One woman got in contact with me after one of my talks to ask me if I could help with her son. He had been arrested during a time when he had a mental health crisis. I wrote a letter to the judge who was responsible for her son's sentencing, using my story as a way to help the judge understand mental illness. My experiences with the criminal justice system were not wasted in the throes of self-pity and regret. I refused to allow myself to get lost in negative emotions. Using the experiences for the good took away most of the lingering shadows of the past.

Her son spent some time in jail but ended up being released. He had recovered and was now well enough to hold a job and have a full life. She said, "Amy, your story allowed me to understand my son's mental challenges. Since I heard your talk, I decided to become a mental health advocate and share our story. You are our champ!" Letters like this served as my fuel to continue my work in raising awareness and coaching other people through difficult circumstances.

~

In January 2020, I had set on a mission to focus on my mind, body, and spirit. As I focused on my body, I was using a Weight Watchers app and following several posts of an upcoming 2020 Wellness Tour by Oprah Winfrey. She was going to be in different cities around the country, holding day long events that focused on mind, body, and spirit wellness. I started following the events and watching her interviews with high profile guests. One in particular that had caught my interest was Lady Gaga.

In Lady Gaga's interview with Oprah, she shared her experience with a psychotic episode. Here was this world-famous celebrity talking about psychosis like many people talk about anxiety. She was unapologetic, transparent, and authentic.

As I watched the interview, I was moved by the fact that I was not alone. It was so rare to hear a celebrity talk about psychosis. Lady Gaga shared that she had been raped as a teenager and that the effects of that tragic experience caused a psychotic break. It shined such a light on my own experience. Finally, I could relate to someone else who was affected by their trauma from childhood as an adult. Recognizing I was not alone provided me with a sense of belonging. It also helped reaffirm to me how important it was to share my story.

In the first week of March, I ended up buying tickets and attending Oprah's 2020 vision tour in Denver, Colorado. I was really lucky to attend the conference because it was held about a week before the pandemic lockdowns. I didn't know what to expect and was surprised to hear Oprah share her story of being sexually abused and how it affected her life. These powerful moments were like a meaningful coincidence that felt like it was meant for me to hear her story. I had a sense of resolution and catharsis. The long struggle I had to recover was finally coming to a triumphant point. I had a feeling of great gratitude and appreciation for everything that led up to that moment. There's something about hearing a person's story that connected me to a deeper level of understanding. It inspired me to share my own story, knowing how much I benefited from realizing I wasn't alone. I wanted to touch someone else's life in a similar way that my life had been touched.

In May 2020, during the pandemic, I continued my advocacy work by reaching people through social media. I conducted live Facebook interviews with people who lived with mental illness. My friend Bill was always eager to hear what I was doing. Our conversations continued to be deep and soulful. We met periodically over lunch in an outdoor park with picnic benches. I asked how much nature had played a role in my recovery journey. My family had a spot in the woods I referred to as God's hotel. It was a mile into the woods from my home. The trees were in abundance, the birds showed up in many colors, and the deer frequently made an appearance in their graceful, elegant ways.

By the fall of 2020, Bill had reached his ninetieth birthday. He asked me, "When are you going to take me to God's hotel and let me see this place you love?" We made a date, and since he didn't drive anymore, I went and picked him up. He was wearing a plaid shirt, tan jacket, and a really cool tan hat. His walking stick was solid oak with a leather strap to support his hand.

We arrived at my house, and he carefully climbed into my Ranger side-by-side. It was a two passenger ATV, which looked like a miniature jeep. His adventurous spirit filled up my heart and brought a tear of joy to my eyes. Bill and I had such a deep connection.

Instead of bringing a picnic lunch, we decided to have grilled hot dogs. We sat in a cleared area under trees that provided umbrella-like shading. He said, "Amy, I need to tell you something."

"You can tell me anything, Bill," I said, leaning forward and sensing he had something very serious to tell me.

"I'm dying. I have cancer in my brain, and I don't have much longer to live," he said straightforwardly. Even though Bill had lived a long life, it was still shocking to hear. I had fully expected Bill to live many more years.

"Ah…Bill. I'm so sorry. I'm going to miss you dearly. I only wish I'd met you sooner, but I'm grateful for all the time we've had together." I could feel a cloud of sadness permeate my body. My eyes teared up, and I got up out of my chair and gave Bill a hug.

"I've had a good life, Amy. I'm really at peace with everything." And then Bill went on to talk about his beliefs of the afterlife.

Three weeks after Bill visited with me, he sent me an email. In the email, he said, "Here's my favorite Irish poem I wanted to give you." The poem was "Bennacht," by John O'Donohue. I took the poem as a message Bill wanted to send to me, that he loved me and wished me all the best.

~

A week later, Bill died. We parted company in the same way we had begun our friendship, with a poem. Every now and then, I read the poem and get a tear in my eye and a smile on my face, as I remember the unconditional love and friendship of a man who helped me to believe in myself again.

After learning Bill died, I had an unexpected flashback. I was able to work through it with relative ease, but I was taken aback at how certain experiences could sometimes be a trigger and surprise me.

Not too long after this happened, I purchased the book *The Body Keeps the Score*. At first when I started reading the book, I found it to be very triggering. It was addressing many topics that made me feel emotionally raw. I really had put the sexual assaults out of my mind for a very long time. The book addressed those topics in details that I really wanted to keep in the back of my mind. I wasn't quite ready to unravel another layer of the complexities of healing.

Although I was fortunate enough to have landed with really exceptional mental health care professionals, I still had to research and learn how to manage my conditions. Bipolar disorder alone requires a deep level of insight and understanding to manage effectively. The effects of trauma are finally showing up in a larger body of research, which means it's trickling into the mainstream vernacular. A greater body of research on trauma has allowed me to understand and heal at a deeper level. It was always important to me to try to make sense of my reactions to what I experienced. I've learned sometimes there are simply no concrete answers, and I've learned to stop asking the question, "Why me?"

I've also learned emergency rooms are probably one of the most ill-equipped places for people with mental illness to turn to for help. In my experience, the healthcare system is often ill-equipped to help someone experiencing a mental health crisis, unless a person is in a city that has a psychiatric emergency room, though that specialized care is not very prevalent. I know there are many other people who have become victims of an ill-equipped system.

I had to come to terms with each piece of my past, which took time and patience. From the sexual assaults, which wreaked havoc with my life, to the interactions with the criminal justice system and a near death experience. One event was quite a bit to cope with; but layered together, it was a lot to process. I tended to focus on one small piece at a time. Each traumatic event had to be processed slowly and carefully, one layer at a time. Healing and grieving weren't a linear process. The memories ebbed and flowed. It seemed that I finally had the skills, experience, and proper support to deal with everything. It helped me tremendously that I believed in recovery. I researched and found many stories of people who had struggled. Their stories shined a light for me that gave me hope I could fully recover, too.

I shed a great deal of gut-wrenching tears, and from time to time fought a battle with suicidal thoughts. Healing was much slower than I would have liked, but eventually I did find peace.

I was fortunate because I was taking medications that prevented me from decompensating to the point where I couldn't function. Instead, I struggled a bit with paranoid thoughts, but my symptoms were transient. It took me a few months to completely recover. I recognized I had come a long way in my recovery journey, but there still were a few triggers. It was a not-so-subtle reminder that I'd never be one hundred percent cured. It was an unsettling reminder of events long past. The shadows of spooky memories would never be gone from my psyche, but I held out hope they'd be in a place where I could retrieve them voluntarily and then put them out of mind, like putting them all in a nice, neat package on a shelf, only taking them out when I wanted to.

~

It was natural to have lots of demands on my schedule, as requests for mental health talks and trainings increased. Keeping myself busy was also one of the healthy ways I coped. In 2021, it was important for me to slow down and reflect on my past. I no longer had any reason to want to avoid uncomfortable feelings and memories. I was at a place where even the most traumatic events were integrated in my memory and could be retrieved without causing me distress. I wasn't afraid of dealing with any emotions that might pop up from my memories. I had come to learn the past was a place to visit, but not a place to stay.

It was good for my mental health to look at pictures and videos I'd made over the years. In the summer of 2008, I had intentionally set out to record my recovery journey. I never expected that journey to last over a decade.

I gave myself a break that it seemed to take me so long to get to a peaceful point. All I ever wanted was to understand myself and have a sense of peace. After everything I'd been through, peace of mind was more precious than any material things I'd ever had.

What I noticed when looking through the photos and videos was there were many different layers to my recovery journey. While it seemed I sure struggled a lot, I also had numerous victories along the way. Sometimes I did take two steps forward and three steps back, but the one thing I never did was give up, even though I admit there were times when I got to the fine line of wanting to quit. I finally stopped telling myself that what happened to me in childhood was "not that bad." Actually, it was bad. I could finally tell the little girl inside of me, "I'm sorry for what happened." It's a small comfort to embrace sorrow and release the pain. Acknowledgement is a powerful salve for deep wounds caused by broken people.

I will never know for certain if I would have experienced flashbacks if I hadn't started sexual abuse therapy in Arizona with Belinda. I don't know the answer. I have learned that when I experienced additional trauma on my life path, it made it more difficult to cope with the traumas from childhood. Before I started seeing Belinda, I had subthreshold PTSD, which means I didn't initially meet the criteria for a diagnosis. But additional traumas, like the interaction with the police and the retraumatizing nature of therapy, made the PTSD more severe.

I also have come to realize several of the mental health care professionals who I encountered were not trained very well in trauma, PTSD, or Complex PTSD, much less being able to effectively treat bipolar disorder too. The mental health care system failed me on more than one occasion and sometimes for a prolonged period of time. The sad thing is I know I'm not alone.

However, outside of the actual traumatic events, the most damaging aspect of sexual assault for me was the cumulative stress of keeping secrets. There's no question the effects of my secrets impacted my mental and physical health. One thing I have learned is if we are silenced, in a sense, we are made invisible. Our experiences are rendered irrelevant and our pain dismissed. I'm no longer willing to accept being silenced and hope there are very few who would vilify me for speaking up.

I stood on numerous stages and shared with audiences how I

strongly believed, even in our lowest points in life, things will always get better. It helped me to have a mom who continuously reinforced this message throughout my life. Her optimism and internal strength permeated my own mind. The strength and determination that was instilled in me at such a young age gave me the resolve to push through some hellacious times in my life. If I ever doubted myself or my capacity to achieve my dreams, I had the great fortune of having a strong-willed mother who reminded me to "think positive," and more than anything, believe my dreams could come true.

The dreams I mapped out while sitting in that Montana jail cell came true. By 2021, I had spoken to or trained over 20,000 people with my mental health advocacy efforts. I became a mental health coach to help others on their recovery journey. Until I sat down to reflect, I had no idea how many people I had reached.

Chapter 20

As I looked back, I pleasantly remembered 2018 as a turning point. It was five years into my journey of being a mental health advocate. There were many people who had taken notice of the impact of my willingness to speak openly about living with a mental illness and the numerous trainings I'd given on mental health. There was a woman from Virginia who had read the book I wrote called *Bipolar Disorder, My Biggest Competitor*. She was so touched by my story that she contacted Libby from NAMI of Greater Wheeling and suggested they nominate me for the Substance Abuse and Mental Health Services (SAMHSA) Voice Award.

For thirteen years, the Voice Awards program honored people in recovery who were improving the lives of people with mental illness, substance use disorders, or both in communities across the country. The awards program also recognized television and film producers that educated the public about behavioral health and showcased that recovery is real and possible through treatment and recovery supports. I had come to learn about several nationally known mental health advocates because they had been recognized by SAMHSA. I found their work inspiring and motivating.

In August 2018, SAMHSA notified me that I was one of the eight consumer/peer leadership nominees for my impact in mental health advocacy. I was really shocked to be recognized for such a prestigious award for my work raising awareness and understanding for mental health.

Although my mom had been with me on my recovery journey, she was unable to travel to California to the campus of UCLA where the award ceremony was held. Instead, Shelley traveled with me to Los Angeles.

When we got to our hotel in Hollywood, I was scanning my memory for the first time I'd seen the memorable Hollywood sign in the hills. I'd made my first trip to California when I was nineteen years old, playing in the National Collegiate Championship basketball tournament for the University of Tennessee. I also spent years working in the California market when I was in the pharmaceutical industry. Yet I had such a different kind of excitement as Shelley and I walked down Hollywood Boulevard, taking pictures of a few select stars on the sidewalk that we found meaningful. I had seen Bob Hope perform, so noting his star was kind of a cool thing. I was emotionally moved with how far I'd come on my recovery journey. I didn't hyperfocus on the past, but I did think about how my life could have been cut short.

The night before the award ceremony, SAMHSA held a banquet with the award winners and invited guests. We were given no advanced notice, but we were asked to share our stories of recovery in front of the fairly large audience. At that point in my life journey, my plan was to use my platform to raise awareness every chance I had for the intersection between people with mental illness and the criminal justice system. It's a very uncomfortable topic and something that's difficult to reveal. But I was convinced changing minds and hearts only starts if someone people can relate to is willing to share their story.

I walked up to the microphone, glanced around the small ballroom, and in a quick moment decided to share my experience of what happened in Montana. My palms were sweating, my heart was beating a bit faster than usual, and my leg was shaking. But I felt compelled to share. In the front of the room sat Kay Warren, a prominent public figure whose son had struggled with mental illness and eventually lost his life by suicide. She had shared her story with the group. I glanced at Kay as I began my talk. She inspired me to have the courage to share.

One of the things I learned after having so many speaking engagements was that people are drawn into the talk with storytelling. When I saw all those people in that audience with their eyes fixated on me, I questioned for a moment why I would ever choose to tell that story. But I did it anyhow.

After giving my talk, I felt uneasy, insecure, and realized I had no control over what people thought of me. Yet I was determined to push through my uncomfortable feelings, believing there was one person in that audience I was speaking directly to. It could have been the one person who had a psychotic episode and felt ashamed, who would know she wasn't alone.

As I sat back down in my seat, one of the gentlemen who sat next to me said, "What a powerful story you have. I'm so glad you shared your experience." I turned and looked at Shelley, and she smiled with approval. The feeling of relief was overwhelming, bringing a sense of peace and tranquility to my mind and body. I felt lighter and happier and more at ease with myself. There were a few people who approached me after the talk and told me how brave I was for sharing my story. It gave me strength to keep pushing forward.

The next evening, we went to the campus of UCLA and the historic eighteen-hundred-seat Royce Hall theatre, where the Voice Awards were held. The theatre was almost completely full. I had butterflies in my stomach as I sat by Shelley a few rows back from the stage. For the most part, it was a "friendly" audience, because everyone knew we were being awarded as people who lived with mental illness or substance use disorders.

We'd been given instructions ahead of time to create about a two-to-three-minute acceptance speech. Earlier that afternoon, I'd sat in the hotel room at the desk and crafted my speech. I contemplated what part of my story I wanted to share. After speaking at the banquet the night before and receiving encouragement, I had the strength to talk about my psychotic episode that led to me being lost in the wilderness. I wanted to demonstrate that people who experience psychosis can and do recover. I mentioned the powerful words the nurse Shirley had said to me in the psych unit in Coeur d'Alene. "You have bipolar disorder, and it's not your fault." I knew there were a lot of people who openly talked about mania and depression, but few who spoke about the common symptom of psychosis that also occurs with a large majority of people who have bipolar disorder. I chose to focus on bipolar disorder because I felt like a discussion about PTSD was much more complicated.

When my introduction was made, the representative from the National Counseling Association highlighted some of my work. I had a quiet, peaceful calm about myself. A sort of internal knowing that what I had accomplished was something I could be proud of. I slowly walked up to the podium, glancing out into the audience and focusing on the friendly faces of my fellow peers. They gave me smiles and nods of encouragement. I set my award down on top of the podium. In a moment of nervousness, I leaned my elbows forward on the podium. I had the kind of joy in my heart that was about as proud as I'd ever been. I'd always been an underdog, but this experience took that attitude to an entirely different level. I'd been in jail, for heaven's sake, and now I was being honored for my work as a mental health advocate. It was a full circle moment like none other.

While it's easy for me to describe in great detail the times I struggled or was hurt, it's much more difficult for me to emotionally connect with joy and happiness. I think I'm a work in progress in reframing my mind to not expect the worst. It's as if I'm almost programmed to expect something bad to happen. My fight or flight response system has been on overdrive for so long, my brain clearly knows how to react to threats. Now, I need to continually learn how to experience joy and perhaps I could do a better job of describing what it felt like to win such a prestigious award.

I could feel a sense of joy and satisfaction that I hadn't felt in a long time. I lifted my head and glanced up at the giant words from the teleprompter. It was a relief knowing I didn't have to memorize my speech.

When the ceremony was over, one of my peers walked up to me and said, "You are so courageous for sharing your story. Thank you." To hear these kind words from a peer made me feel like I had used the platform in a positive way. I was incredibly grateful to have that chance to use something challenging for the good.

It was rather ironic the award I received was called the "Voice Award." From the days I spent talking on video camera to the time I stood on that stage and accepted the award, I had traveled, quite literally, long and far. As I stood on that stage and looked out at the audience, I had felt so much joy inside. It was as if I'd known all along I'd be standing on a stage for one reason or another and speaking my truth. Even during moments of doubt and uncertainty, my inner voice never wavered, reminding me of the importance of staying true to myself and what I believed in.

The event was streamed live on the Internet, so my family and friends tuned in to watch. A few days after I was back home, I received an email from a woman who watched the ceremony. She said, "Thank you for sharing your story. I sat with my son, who has bipolar disorder, watching, and your talk gave him so much hope. I can't thank you enough."

I didn't know if there was anyone else who may have been impacted by the words I said on that stage. It really didn't matter to me how many people; it only mattered that I knew of one. And the fact that one person was helped by me sharing my story gave me the fuel I needed to keep on sharing.

Even though secrecy and silence had at one time festered into something I didn't deserve, I recognized there was nothing I could do to change the past. Instead, I decided to focus on how I might be able to do just a little bit of good by sharing my truth. I was a long way from all the pain and struggle of having to relive all the trauma that was inflicted on me. No more trembling and shaking with flashbacks. I was for sure living in the present moment.

I measure my healing journey in many ways. One that stands out in my mind is being connected to my emotions and my ability to not only feel sadness, but also feel joy and happiness. I am no longer numbing my emotions as a way to cope. I'm not afraid of the ghosts from the past. Sometimes it seems all I've lived through happened to another person. I'm so far away from being the distraught woman lying in the desert dirt. And yet I've been able to tap into a level of compassion for myself and others that I may otherwise never had if it weren't for that experience. I've been able to truly appreciate the power of being in the present moment. And I make a point of allowing myself to be inspired by others.

I have a great appreciation and respect for storytelling. As This is My Brave co-founder Jennifer Marshall always says, "Storytelling saves lives!" I'm hopeful that by writing this book I'll find the one person who needed to hear this story. Maybe, just maybe, they'll become *Unsilenced,* too.

Acknowledgements

When I sat down in January 2023 to write "Unsilenced," I was blessed to have my biggest cheerleader and supporter, my mother by my side. I finished the first draft in August, and my mom passed away September 5, 2023. She was able to see the cover and read most of what I had written. She is one of the reasons why I was able to have such a strong voice. Her consistent love, encouragement and understanding gave me a tremendous amount of inspiration. She told me to be sure I went to the local library and talk about my book. I said, "It won't be the same without you." She replied, "I'll be with you in spirit." So, mom my guardian angel, thanks for everything and I do mean everything! You'll always be with me.

One of the biggest reasons I was able to have the confidence to get my words on the page is because I had an awesome book coach, Maurene Janiece (maurenejaniece.com). I began writing this book using a storyboard. After a few days of putting my vision together, I knew I needed a coach to help me with the technical aspect of storytelling and for support and encouragement. I had never worked with a book coach before, but I had lots of experiences in coaching others and being coached in athletics. Maurene exceeded all of my expectations. She rolled up her sleeves and helped me bring my story to life. Her overall professionalism and knowledge about story telling was exceptional. Even though I was grappling with many taboo topics, Maurene never wavered. I couldn't have asked for a better coach. Thank you, Maurene for pouring your heart and soul into coaching me. I'm forever grateful to you!

When I wrote my second book, "Bipolar Disorder, My Biggest Competitor," I reached out to one of my childhood friends who edited the book for me. Since that time, Lori Whitwam (furwoodforest.blog) has continued to establish herself internationally as a "go to" editor for Indie authors. She's always involved in the story and helps to polish the manuscript. Thank you Lori for being my editor (again), my friend and another one of my encouragers when my self-doubt got in the way.

While I was writing my book, my sister Shelley was diagnosed with endometrial cancer. She ended up staying with me for a couple of months while she recovered. Lucky for me this meant she was part of the captive audience for reviewing words I'd written, the cover design, the blurb and my website. Shelley fully recovered and was there when I finished my first draft. Thanks Shelley, for being there for me, reassuring me when I questioned myself and for just being a good sister.

My techie niece Natalie provided support and encouragement. She took time out of her busy schedule and reviewed everything from the cover design to early reading of the first chapter. Her creativity and inspiration served me well on my journey to complete "Unsilenced." Thank you, Natalie!

A big thank you to the people who I provided Advanced Review Copies. Special thanks to Monica Leppma for all the feedback and encouragement. A huge thank you to my Lady Vol forever sister, Linda Vittetoe. Your kindness and authentic encouragement really meant the world to me. To my dear friend Charlotte Carpenter, you are truly a spiritual blessing in my life.

Lastly, thank you to my readers. I know you have many choices in how to spend your time, I'm so grateful you decided to spend your time reading my book. My hope is it may have helped you in some way. If you'd like to connect with me, you can reach me at www.amygambleauthor.com

About the Author

Amy Gamble is a national award-winning Mental Health Advocate, a 1988 Olympian in the sport of Team Handball and a mental health coach. Amy graduated from the University of Arizona with a degree in the Communication of Behavioral Sciences. She also has a graduate degree in Organizational Behavior.

If you'd like to subscribe to Amy's monthly author newsletter you can sign-up at www.amygambleauthor.com